Additional Praise for *Paul Volcker:*

The Making of a Financial Legend

"As Joseph Treaster's quite wonderful biography makes clear, Paul Volcker is a rare gift to the nation. Read this book and be reminded anew of the extraordinary integrity and intellectual firepower Volcker has made synonymous with his service to the Republic. You may not think you care about the role of the Federal Reserve, but after you read *Paul Volcker: The Making of a Financial Legend*, you will."

–Hodding Carter III,
State Department Spokesman
in the Carter Administration
and currently President of the John S.
and James L. Knight Foundation

"I remember well when Paul Volcker became chairman of the Fed and vowed to break inflation. Not many believed him, but he did it, almost single-handedly. The story of this great financial strategist will help you understand today's economy and what lies ahead."

–Jim Rogers, international investor
and author of the bestselling books,
Adventure Capitalist
and *Investment Biker*

"Through five decades of competence and integrity in both the public and private sectors, Paul Volcker has gained the respect of the world's financial leaders while never forgetting those in America who needed a helping hand. He has been the voice of calm in times of financial crisis and of innovation in times of opportunity. Above all he has been candid in a world where candor often takes second place to public relations and spin. Treaster's compelling book about an extraordinary American is long overdue."

–Former Senator Bill Bradley

PAUL
VOLCKER

THE MAKING OF A
FINANCIAL LEGEND

JOSEPH B. TREASTER

WILEY

John Wiley & Sons, Inc.

Published by John Wiley & Sons, Inc., Hoboken, New Jersey
Published simultaneously in Canada

For general information on our other products and services, or technical support, please contact our Customer Care Department within the United States at 800-762-2974, outside the United States at 317-572-3993 or fax 317-572-4002.

Wiley also publishes its books in a variety of electronic formats. Some content that appears in print may not be available in electronic books.

For more information about Wiley products, visit our web site at *www.wiley.com*.

Library of Congress Cataloging-in-Publication Data:

Treaster, Joseph B.
  Paul Volcker : the making of a financial legend / Joseph B. Treaster.
    p. cm.
  Includes bibliographical references and index.
  ISBN 0-471-42812-4 (cloth)
  1. Volcker, Paul A. 2. Economists–United States–Biography. 3. Board of Governors of the Federal Reserve System (U.S.)–Officials and employees–Biography. 4. United States–Economic policy–1971–1981. 5. United States–Economic policy–1981–1993. I. Title.
  HB119.V6T74 2004
  332.1'1'092–dc22

                                                                      2004000250

Printed in the United States of America

10 9 8 7 6 5 4 3 2 1

To Barbara and Chloe,
my true loves

Contents

Foreword

Without Paul Volcker's toughness and guts, we may never have broken the grip of rising inflation and declining productivity that plagued the United States during the 1970s. And we surely would not have been positioned to enjoy record economic growth in the 1990s. It would have been amazing to think in 1982, but now inflation barely registers as a concern in the United States. For that, Americans have to thank Paul Volcker.

At the start of the 1980s, America was suffering through its greatest economic crisis since I was a young boy during the Great Depression. In March of 1982, as Chairman of the American Stock Exchange, I put forward Wall Street's perspective on President Reagan's economic policies in an address at the National Press Club in Washington, buttressing my remarks with data from a poll of 400 leaders in the financial community. The results of the poll, conducted by the Exchange, were clear: Business leaders were losing enthusiasm for the president's economic plans, but they overwhelmingly supported Paul Volcker's stewardship of monetary policy at the Federal Reserve Board.

At the time, that was not an opinion shared by most Americans. As Joseph Treaster vividly describes in the following pages, Volcker was under intense pressure to reverse his policy of monetary restraint. At the time, it was hard for a lot of people to see that Volcker was administering the medicine that our ailing economy sorely needed. But I believed that he was. That is why at the end of that talk at the National Press Club, I told the reporters there that Volcker "may be the only voice of sanity left in Washington. We respect him for his toughness and guts." My comments elicited a small storm of controversy, but I stood by them then, and I stand by them now.

Having gotten to know Paul over the years, I can say that this courage is a manifestation of how he has lived his personal and professional life. He has always stood for what he believes is right, regardless of the political consequences.

After Volcker left the Fed, he undertook the difficult task of chairing a joint committee of Jewish groups and Swiss banks to bring resolution to the question of unclaimed accounts of Holocaust victims. It was a situation fraught with emotion and acrimony, one in which the chance for failure was high. Yet Volcker took on the task, oversaw a massive accounting of Swiss bank records, and helped force a $1.25 billion agreement.

As that process was winding down in 2002, Volcker answered the call at Arthur Andersen, agreeing to chair an independent oversight committee at the height of that accounting firm's problems concerning the Enron collapse. It was a total no-win situation. The public was outraged at the firm's role in this massive corporate scandal, and the accounting industry had a history of obstinacy toward reform.

But Volcker truly believed that it was important to the future of accounting and to the future of our market system for him to help turn Arthur Andersen into a model for the entire field. Unfortunately, Volcker's reorganization plan was never implemented, as criminal indictments quickly doomed the future of Arthur Andersen. Yet many of the recommendations that Volcker made—such as restrictions on nonaudit work and the rotation of auditors—became part of the groundbreaking Sarbanes-Oxley Act passed by Congress later that year.

Finally, I saw Volcker's courage up close as a fellow member of the Conference Board's Blue-Ribbon Commission on Public Trust and Private Enterprise. When everyone else in this august group of business leaders was talking about the right formula to treat stock options as an expense—an important move to realign the interests of management and shareholders—Volcker took the practical, principled, and bold stand that these options should be banned outright.

What motivates Volcker to take these principled stands is engagingly detailed in the following chapters. Joseph Treaster's book paints an encompassing portrait of one of the great economic minds and financial leaders of our time, detailing his professional triumphs as well as the personal side of the man, from his upbringing in New Jersey to his struggles in caring for his wife and family.

Reading this book, one also learns the story of a now rare breed: the private sector leader who takes his public obligations seriously.

In an era in which business leaders are celebrated on magazine covers for acquiring a company in one stroke of the pen, firing tens of thousands of employees in another stroke, and in yet another, selling off the enterprise years later for less than shareholders paid for it in the first place, Volcker stands out as an exception to the rule. He traded years of lucrative earnings on Wall Street for years in the public service, and, when he moved to the private sector, placed more value on maintaining his integrity than on maintaining a flashy lifestyle.

Now, when anyone is drawing up a list of people to head an important public commission, Paul Volcker heads the list. Unfortunately, he is often the only name on it. Today, there are too few private sector leaders who appreciate the responsibilities that they have to the rest of society, who understand that their expertise is needed to navigate the challenges before us, and who recognize that their interests are served when they serve the public interest.

I hope those reading this book will see the story of Paul Volcker's life not only as a piece of history, but as an example of the type of public-spirited behavior we need from our business leaders in the years to come. I can think of no more fitting tribute to this great man.

Arthur Levitt, Jr.
Westport, Connecticut
March 2004

CHAPTER ONE

A FINANCE LEGEND

The lanky man in the rumpled suit puffed serenely on a cigar, and the members of the House Committee on Banking sputtered with rage. The lawmakers had been flooded by their constituents with heartbreaking stories of personal hardship as the nation slid ever deeper into the worst recession since the Great Depression. Interest rates had shot above 20 percent, millions of Americans had been thrown out of work, and consumer spending had plummeted. The vital industries that built and sold homes and cars were struggling, and thousands of businesses were heading into bankruptcy.

Yet, as the Congressmen questioned the one man most responsible for the hard times, Paul A. Volcker Jr., the chairman of the Federal Reserve Board, they drew no comfort. As bad as conditions were, Volcker said on that summer day in 1981, they were only going to get worse.[1]

Volcker knew, because he pulled the levers and pressed the buttons that largely determined the flow of money in

America, whether it would be bountiful or scarce and how much it would cost to borrow. He had deliberately orchestrated a stratospheric rise in interest rates over the previous two years in a determined campaign to crush inflation. He had not expected interest rates to soar quite so high or the economy to fall quite so deeply into distress,[2] but he was convinced that the constant escalation of prices—the essence of inflation—gravely threatened America's economic stability and its status as a world leader, and that it had to be stopped.

Most Americans, however, did not see the danger. As troubled as they were by the uncertainties of ever rising prices, they had learned to live with inflation. They realized that the money in their pockets was losing value every month, so they bought homes and land that would rise in value as inflation rose and took out loans that would be paid back in inflated dollars. They demanded and received higher wages. Manufacturers marked up their goods. When Volcker slammed on the brakes and threw the economy into a dive, the country was stunned—and many Americans complained to their representatives in Washington.

Calm and seemingly detached in a wreath of wispy cigar smoke, Volcker told the Congressmen in their grand hearing room that summer day that while he saw signs that inflation was declining, he was cutting back further on the supply of money in the economy,[3] knowing that almost certainly business failures would multiply and millions more would lose their jobs. He was doing this, he said, for the long-term good of the country.

The Congressmen literally shrieked. Frank Annunzio, a Democrat from Illinois, shouted and pounded his desk.[4] "Your course of action is wrong," he yelled, his voice breaking with emotion. "It must be wrong. There isn't anybody who says you're right."[5] Volcker's high interest rates were "destroying the small businessman," decried George Hansen, a Republican from Idaho.[6] "We're destroying Middle America," Representative Hansen said. "We're destroying the American Dream." Representative Henry B. Gonzalez, a Democrat from Texas, called for Volcker's impeachment, saying he had permitted big banks to be "predatory dinosaurs that suck up billions of dollars in resources" to support mergers while doing little to help neighborhood stores and workshops and the average American consumer.[7]

The outburst was a distillation of national sentiment—or resentment—that would only deepen as unemployment rose to a high of nearly 11 percent and interest rates, which peaked the following month in August 1981 at 20½ percent, remained close to 16 percent for the next year.

As the recession worsened, Americans beseeched Volcker to relent. Building contractors and carpenters inundated his offices in Washington with stubby lengths of two-by-fours, lumber they said they would not need since no one was buying houses. They slapped mailing labels on the wood and scrawled plaintive messages. On one block now sitting on a shelf at the Federal Reserve, Lloyd Fancett wrote, "I need my job, don't stop housing." L. D. Estes Jr., of Texarkana, Arkansas, sent in a block with a knothole. "Dear Mr. Volcker," he wrote in black marker, "I am beginning to feel as useless as this knothole. Where will our children live?"

Car dealers sent Volcker mailbags full of ignition keys for sedans and coupes that had no buyers. Farmers brought their tractors to the capital and paraded gloomily around the Federal Reserve headquarters, along Constitution Avenue, up 21st Street, then back on C Street. Some of the protests were menacing. In Kentucky, a homebuilders' association tacked up "Wanted" posters featuring Volcker and the six other Federal Reserve governors. In neighboring Tennessee, a building trades magazine accused Volcker and his colleagues of the "premeditated and cold-blooded murder of millions of small businesses" and of "kidnapping (and holding for ransom) the American dream of home ownership."[8] Shortly before Christmas, a man talked his way into the Federal Reserve, dashed up the interior marble stairs, and got as far as a closed-door meeting in the majestic Federal Reserve boardroom before he was tackled by a guard. The man, who told the police he was upset about high interest rates, was carrying a sawed-off shotgun, a pistol, a knife, and a satchel containing a fake bomb.[9]

Volcker's fight against inflation had consequences even the Fed chairman could not have predicted, contributing strongly to the defeat of President Carter in 1980 and significantly hurting the popularity of his successor, Ronald Reagan. Both presidents chose not to quarrel openly with Volcker, but their aides felt less constrained, with some of the more pronounced hectoring coming from President Reagan's Treasury secretaries, Donald T. Regan and James A. Baker III, who earlier had served as White House chief of staff. When Volcker told President Reagan in the summer of 1987 that he was resigning, Baker could not contain his glee. "We got the son of a bitch," Baker told a friend in New York.[10]

—

Volcker ultimately defeated inflation, putting the country on the path to its greatest run of prosperity in history. In recognition of his success and his unyielding adherence to principles and tactics, his stature has risen to the level of demigod in the world of economics and finance. "If you play free association with the name Paul Volcker, two words come up, integrity and steadfastness," says Alan S. Blinder, a Princeton University economics professor who served on President Bill Clinton's Council of Economic Advisers and was Clinton's appointee as vice chairman of the Federal Reserve Board in 1994.[11]

Alan Greenspan, the current chairman of the Fed, hails Volcker as the father of America's economic vitality over most of the last two decades and says his own success in driving down inflation to historic lows has been largely an extension of "the basic policy that Volcker put in place."[12]

Volcker's approach to tackling inflation has its detractors, but even they acknowledge his historic achievement and admire his iron will. Nobel laureate in economics Joseph E. Stiglitz views him with "enormous respect,"[13] even though he believes Volcker inflicted more pain than necessary on America.

Likewise, Professor Blinder would have preferred a slower pace in the inflation fight, but heralds the results. In the years since Volcker administered his shock therapy, Blinder points out, inflation has been "a very minor social and economic issue in this country."[14] As Volcker saw it, he had to strike hard to jolt Americans out of the expectation that prices would inevitably leapfrog higher and that the only way to stay ahead was to keep spending and demanding higher pay.[15]

In retrospect, Greenspan says, Volcker may not have needed to apply as much pressure as he did, but there was no way for Volcker or anyone else to know that. The inflation he faced was like a virulent cancer. In a situation like that, Greenspan says, one tends toward overdose. "You do not want to take the chance that you will underdose," he says, "because you might not get a second chance."[16]

—

Volcker was probably the best-prepared chairman ever to preside over the Federal Reserve, both in education and manner of thinking. But for all his brilliance in setting monetary policy and skill in navigating Washington politics, he often came across to ordinary Americans as a cold and arrogant numbers cruncher. The ever present cigar only reinforced the public's perception of him as a hard-nosed banker's banker. In a way, that's what he was. But he was convinced that he had to act decisively to save his country from ruin. His predecessors had tried to dampen inflation, but had retreated as Americans began to feel the pain. The result had been an exceedingly long, rippling upward climb of inflation. Volcker, the son of a revered town manager dedicated to public service, felt a duty to stay the course. "If he would have walked away from it, it would have really endangered the United States," says Henry Kaufman, Volcker's colleague and friend from the early days at the Fed and for years the head of research at Salomon Brothers on Wall Street.[17]

Conversations with Kaufman and veterans of Volcker's war on inflation, including Volcker himself, make clear that there was never any question of his turning back. The Fed chairman and his lieutenants were like surgeons working on a patient, though Volcker admits he "did a lot of pacing the floor."[18] Volcker compares himself to a physician administering medicine: "The doctor says, 'I know you don't like this, but it's good for you.' Maybe that sounds trivial. But you don't do it unless you think it's for the overall good of the country."[19]

—

Paul Volcker is regarded as one of the world's great economic strategists. But he is much more than that. He is also an instinctive leader, a figure of unshakable integrity and that almost unheard-of master of Wall Street and Washington finance who has never sought to amass personal wealth. At 76, he continues, by Wall Street standards, to live modestly.

Since his departure from the Fed almost two decades ago, Volcker has remained engaged in both the financial world and the world at large, striving most recently to revive the Arthur Andersen accounting firm and to recover billions in lost savings of Holocaust victims from Swiss banks. This book is the story of his half-century of service and an account of the enormous impact he has had on American business and finance, and on the lives of the more than 290 million Americans.

CHAPTER TWO

SEVENTY-SIX

After three decades of government service, Paul Volcker stepped down from the Federal Reserve in 1987, feeling younger than his nearly 60 years and showing no signs of shifting to a slower pace. With little fanfare, he galloped off to begin a new career as a university professor and a New York City investment banker. Yet he never stopped seeing himself as a public servant, and in the next phase of his life his unpaid work in pursuit of corporate honesty, a strengthened civil service, and aid to the victims of the Holocaust far overshadowed his private business career. As corporate scandals at Enron, the huge Texas-based energy trading company, and the missteps of the world's biggest accounting and consulting firms unfolded in the early years of the new century, Volcker emerged more than ever as a beacon of integrity and strength, a legend of finance whose solid principles never yielded.

Thriftiness and unpretentiousness are as much a part of Volcker as his towering 6-foot, 7-inch frame. He seemed to delight in cheap cigars and bargain suits and he has always found it difficult to discard a shirt just because it was beginning to fray. When he became president of the Federal Reserve Bank in New York, he immediately replaced the official limousine with a standard sedan.

Though his work has profoundly affected the financial well-being of millions of Americans, he has never placed much emphasis on his own personal riches. By his account, he has ambled though life without a career plan and, by all appearances, has had no greater goal than doing the best job he could in the public interest. Though Volcker is nominally a Democrat who admires Harry Truman and Adlai Stevenson, his style has generally been nonpartisan. The result of all this has been that public and private organizations have been powerfully drawn to him in times of need. Alan S. Blinder, the Princeton University economics professor and former vice chairman of the Federal Reserve Board, calls Volcker "an exemplar of the notion of public service."[1]

As he celebrated his 76th birthday in 2003, Volcker had accumulated a comfortable reserve of money. Yet he stuck to his lifelong low-budget daily routine, occasionally riding a New York City public bus and walking a few blocks to his small office in Rockefeller Center. He had long ago given up his favorite Antonio y Cleopatra cigars for health reasons, but he had begun thinking they were getting expensive when they got up to a quarter apiece.

In his prime, as chairman of the Fed in the 1980s, Volcker appeared on the covers of *Time* and *Newsweek*, regularly came into American living rooms on the nightly television news, and was often referred to as the second most powerful person in America, with only the president regarded as having more clout. Volcker was the go-to guy on the economy. And the reputation born out of his term as chairman remains constant to this day.

—

As the fever of corporate scandal spread over America in recent years, Volcker was in heavy demand. Senators and representatives called him to Washington to testify before Congress. He was often mentioned as a candidate for important government and regulatory posts.

One of the central themes in the Enron disaster was deception through accounting. Arthur Andersen, an accounting and consulting giant with annual revenue of $9 billion, 1,750 partners, and 80,000 employees, was Enron's auditor. Disturbing reports about the two companies filled the newspapers and the airwaves. In early January of 2002, with investigations by the Securities and Exchange Commission, the Justice Department, and Congress under way, lawyers for Andersen made a stunning discovery. As they prepared testimony before Congress,[2] the lawyers found that a large number of potentially incriminating e-mail messages and computer files dealing with Enron had been deleted. They found signs, too, that many documents had been shredded. Eventually, investigators would determine that Andersen had destroyed roughly 30,000 e-mail messages and computer files and nearly a ton of paper documents relating to the troubled energy company.[3]

In a business based on trust, Andersen was in extreme trouble. With the firm's reputation in ruins, its chief executive, Joseph F. Berardino, went looking for a savior. He sought to create an independent board to demonstrate that

Andersen intended to make a fresh start. To lead the board, he needed someone with impeccable credentials—someone like Paul Volcker. "We're in big trouble," Volcker recalls Berardino saying.[4] "We've got to make some changes." Berardino was looking for someone to steer the firm in a new direction. "It was more than oversight in the sense of just approving what they were doing," Volcker says, "but it wasn't running the place in the sense of operating it, day by day."[5]

Volcker was intrigued, but in order to accept the position he wanted full authority to make whatever changes he deemed necessary, including the replacement of Berardino and other senior executives. "He went away and a few days later sent me an e-mail on what they had in mind; he'd obviously consulted with friends," Volcker says. "And it was weak, and I said, 'Well, if that's what you've got in mind, I'm not interested.' So he came back saying, 'Oh, no. No. No. You tell us what you've got in mind.'"

Volcker reiterated his conditions, and on February 3, Andersen announced from its headquarters in Chicago that Volcker had agreed to become chairman of an independent oversight board to work with the firm "in making fundamental changes in its audit practices."[6] The company also said it was taking steps to reduce conflicts of interest and specified wide-ranging powers for Volcker.

Accounting professionals were amazed. "What they've done now is almost hard to believe," Arthur W. Bowman, the editor of *Bowman's Accounting Report,* told Jonathan Glater of *The New York Times.*[7] "They're going to give this committee carte blanche to make recommendations, and they'll follow them without question."

Volcker, who declined, as usual, to be paid for his services, was not so sure it would work out that crisply. But he expected to be able to bring substantial change to Andersen. Otherwise, he said, "I could not possibly invite other people to join this board."[8]

Volcker did not know at the time that he had not been Berardino's first choice. Arthur Levitt, the former chairman of the Securities and Exchange Commission, was among the others Berardino considered before seeking out Volcker, but Volcker says that would not have mattered. He saw an opportunity to directly affect what he regarded as the declining standards of American accounting firms, and he was not about to let pride stand in the way. Nearly two years earlier he had become chairman of the board of trustees of the International Accounting Standards Committee Foundation in London, the parent of a board that has developed auditing rules followed by many countries. He was particularly concerned that lucrative consulting contracts posed a conflict of interest for the accounting firms. The danger was that to get the consulting fees the firms could be tempted to compromise on the accounting. In 2000, Enron paid Andersen $27 million in consulting fees, $2 million more than the $25 million it paid the firm for auditing.[9]

In the crisis at Andersen, Volcker saw a chance to retool one of the giants of accounting, turning it into an incubator for a purer kind of auditing. Competitive pressure, he believed, would force other firms to follow Andersen's lead. For Volcker, that was the big draw. "I thought it was a good lever for getting Andersen reformed, and through Andersen, setting a model for the industry, for the profession," Volcker says.[10]

To work with him on the independent oversight board, Volcker recruited Charles A. Bowsher, a former comptroller general of the United States and head of the General Accounting Office, the investigative arm of Congress; P. Roy Vagelos, a former chief executive of Merck & Company; and a handful of others including John C. Bogle, the retired chairman and founder of the Vanguard Group, and Russell E. Palmer, a former dean of the Wharton School at the University of Pennsylvania.

Before the group could get under way, Volcker learned in early March that the prosecutors were preparing to indict Andersen within days. "At that point," he says, "we got together much faster than we otherwise would have and put out a document as to how we would like to see Andersen reformed."[11] The idea was to show the prosecutors an alternative: "Look, we're going to have a reformed firm. You don't have to indict it."[12] In a news conference in New York on March 11, Volcker proposed breaking apart Andersen's accounting and auditing businesses, separating them into independent companies with no sharing of revenue.[13] Under Volcker's plan, no auditor would be in charge of overseeing a client's books for more than five years, to reduce the chance of personal relationships clouding judgments. He also recommended a "cooling-off" period of a year before partners could accept jobs with accounting clients and called for the elimination of bonuses for auditors who persuaded clients to buy consulting services.[14]

Volcker was in such a rush to make the plan public that he announced it before his panel of advisers could review it. But his efforts were undercut by a phlegmatic response from Andersen. Charlie Leonard, a spokesman for the firm, told a reporter for *The Washington Post*, "We appreciate his hard work."[15] Leonard assured *The Wall Street Journal* that Volcker's recommendations would "be seriously reviewed."[16]

But the Justice Department was looking for much more from Andersen. It was going to take a significant show of contrition on the accounting firm's part, not merely a pledge to begin following pristine practices. On March 14, Andersen was indicted for obstruction of justice.

A week later, Volcker abandoned subtleties. This time when he called reporters together in a news conference, his pitch to the Justice Department was direct and to the point. He and six other financial experts would take control of Andersen and replace the firm's top executives, providing the prosecutors dropped their criminal case.[17] He said several other things would have to happen before his group would take the reins of Andersen. But the key, "the most fundamental stumbling block," as Volcker puts it, "was the indictment."[18]

With the indictment facing Andersen, the firm was essentially doomed. "They weren't going to have any clients left," Volcker says. "Being accused of being criminally derelict is not a conducive atmosphere for retaining clients."

New York Times reporter Jonathan Glater got mixed reaction from Andersen on Volcker's plan to take charge of the firm.[19] Charlie Leonard said it was "clear that Mr. Volcker has broad authority," but added that it was also clear that Berardino, Andersen's chief executive, was "the elected CEO of the worldwide organization." Leonard's colleague at Andersen, Patrick Dorton, was more upbeat. "This is a positive and constructive proposal that works to resolve the difficult issues with the SEC, the Department of Justice, and other claimants," he told Glater. In a conversation that day with a reporter for *The Washington Post,* Volcker said: "It is a confused company at the moment; they're trying to decide whether to live or die."[20]

The Justice Department did not immediately say no, but it offered little hope of a deal. Meaningful reform would certainly be kept in mind as prosecutors weighed indicting Andersen, said Brian Sierra, a Justice Department spokesman.[21] But cooperation with investigators and the full acceptance of responsibility were also important. This was a crucial gap Volcker could not bridge. The prosecutors were sure of their case and Andersen's partners were just as firmly convinced that a jury would see the case their way: That the company was a victim of overzealous prosecutors. There was no give. Andersen had already entered a not guilty plea and was preparing for trial on May 6.[22]

Less than two weeks after the indictment, Joseph Berardino was gone, announcing his resignation on March 26 and leaving Andersen without a chief executive. Andersen's lawyers kept talking to the prosecutors and in early April, according to Kurt Eichenwald of *The New York Times,* they came close to a deal. But on April 6, David B. Duncan, the senior Andersen auditor on the Enron account, pleaded guilty to a felony and agreed to testify against the firm. There was one more round of settlement talks, but that, too, failed.[23]

Even before then, Volcker had lost hope. As he saw it, the firm had become totally paralyzed.[24] He was never able to get "a critical mass" of partners to sign on to his changes. "There were a good number that were ready to go along," he says, "but a lot of the others just wanted to get the hell out."

On May 5, the weekend before the Andersen trial was to begin in Houston, Volcker issued a brief statement that he was suspending his work with the firm. "We had stopped being active some time before that," Volcker says.[25] "But I didn't want to make an announcement. It wasn't my position to apply the coup de grâce. I would have been shooting a dead man. The guy already had three bullets in his lungs. I didn't need to put another bullet in his head."

On June 15 Andersen was convicted of obstruction of justice, and within a few hours the Securities and Exchange Commission announced that the firm had agreed that by August 31 it would stop auditing publicly traded companies. In September the firm was sentenced to five years of probation and fined $500,000, the maximum penalty under Federal law. [26]

The scandal at Andersen cost thousands of employees their jobs and reduced competition among big accounting firms. But the prosecutors were convinced they had served the nation well by firing a cannon shot that would forever reverberate in the minds of American executives as they contemplated how far they were willing to push legal and moral limits in pursuit of corporate growth and personal wealth.

—

In retrospect, Volcker was probably overly optimistic about the future of the firm. At one point, talking with Louis Uchitelle of *The New York Times* during his work at Andersen, Volcker referred to himself mockingly as Don Quixote. But his work was not fruitless. Though he was not able to rescue Andersen, some of the changes he advocated were incorporated by Congress a few months later in some of the most sweeping securities legislation since the 1930s. Volcker was not the only one calling for new standards. But the Andersen post created heightened visibility for Volcker and his views, and amplified his themes for the lawmakers in Washington.

The reform legislation, written by Senator Paul S. Sarbanes, a Democrat from Maryland, and Representative Michael G. Oxley, an Ohio Republican, and promptly signed by President George W. Bush, not only adopted Volcker's proposed restrictions on consulting and the rotation of lead auditors, but, in direct response to Andersen, broadened the definition of document destruction and doubled the criminal penalties for individuals to up to 20 years in prison. The new law required chief executives and chief financial officers, for the first time, to personally certify quarterly and annual financial reports, prohibited most corporate loans to senior executives, and prevented executives from filing for bankruptcy to avoid paying fines for violations of securities laws. It also increased protections for whistle-blowers.

One of the strongest provisions of the Sarbanes-Oxley Act overrode the long-standing objections of the accounting industry to the creation of an independent regulatory body that would set standards and discipline auditors. For the auditors, self-regulation was over. The new organization, the Public Company Accounting Oversight Board, would come under the purview of the Securities and Exchange Commission, which would choose the chairman and four members of the board. The first choice for chairman was Paul Volcker.[27]

For several weeks, Volcker debated whether to accept the

post. It was an opportunity to go far beyond leading by example at Andersen. As chairman of the accounting oversight board, Volcker would dictate the behavior of the accounting profession and be armed with the authority to punish rogues. He would also have a bully pulpit for his other passions in corporate management. Volcker particularly wanted to eliminate stock options (contracts to buy stock at a predetermined price) as part of executive pay packages. Stock options become valuable only if a company's stock rises, and Volcker regarded them as dangerous incentives for executives to employ any tactic—even illegal ones—to drive share prices higher. He also wanted to reduce the power of American chief executives by requiring them to relinquish the chairmanship of the board to an executive with no ties to the company—a nonexecutive chairman, selected by the board with confirmation by the vote of shareholders.

Congress provided that financing for the accounting oversight board would come from fees collected from all but the smallest of publicly traded companies and that the chairman would receive a huge annual salary of $556,000[28]— more than President George W. Bush's salary and nearly four times the $142,500 annual pay of the chairman of the board's parent agency, the Securities and Exchange Commission.[29] Typically for Volcker, the money was not a key factor. More enticing was the proposal that while the board's headquarters would be in Washington, he would also be able to have an office in New York.[30] Yet in the end, Volcker decided against the assignment in favor of his other projects.[31] He was, without doubt, fully engaged, putting in long days at his office in New York and frequently on the road, in the United States and around the world. He was an adviser to a Japanese bank and several international corporations, a member of the small trust committees that guided the management of the family fortunes of the Rockefellers and the Kennedys and the chairman or a trustee of more than a dozen nonprofit organizations. But none of those jobs was as highly visible or likely to have the long-term significance of the one he declined. "I think he made a mistake," says Michael Bradfield, a lawyer who has worked with Volcker for more than 30 years.[32] "It would have been good for him. He likes to have more to do than it's possible to do. He likes to run a big organization and he likes to be confronted with big problems that require big answers. That's why I thought it was the right job."

While Congress was discussing the creation of the accounting oversight board during the summer of 2002, Volcker argued in testimony that the chairmanship should be part time. But with corporate America unraveling, the lawmakers were in no mood for half-measures. "My conception was, you've got a very strong executive director, you didn't need a fulltime board," Volcker says.[33] "It had to be an active board, but it didn't need to be full-time. And the chairman himself would not be full-time. Under those conditions, I would have taken it."

At one point in conversation with me, Volcker seemed to suggest that he passed up the opportunity because he thought he might be losing his fast ball, and that over a tenure of three or four years at the accounting board he might start throwing more balls than strikes. "I was conscious that I was 75 years old," Volcker said.[34] Yes, he was getting up there in years, but even as we spoke in late 2003 and he had celebrated his 76th birthday, he was still charging around at a pace that would have winded most 50-year-olds.

—

I caught sight of Volcker loping down Lexington Avenue near his apartment one morning in the fall of 2003, a slightly hunched figure in an old trench coat and brown fedora, moving at flank speed. He flashed past the window, staring straight ahead in the direction of his office, his doughy face frozen in concentration. This was no pensioner out for a stroll, perhaps thinking the exercise might do him good. This was Paul Volcker, hammer down, plunging hell-bent toward his next meeting, a running back in mufti. This was not the picture of a man running out of steam. This was a man with all the tools: the brains, the stamina, and the status. I asked him every way I could think of if there were some other reason he declined the accounting board job. But Volcker, being Volcker, responded the same way: "I just didn't, that's the answer, I didn't want to give up everything else, whether it was right or wrong."

—

To accept the accounting board assignment, Volcker would have had to sacrifice his work on behalf of Holocaust victims. But as he was considering the post late in the summer of 2002, the most difficult and most important aspects of his Holocaust mission had been accomplished, and he had turned over all but the last threads of responsibility to his old friend and colleague, Michael Bradfield, a lawyer who had worked with him at the Treasury Department and the Federal Reserve.

By then, Volcker had been immersed in the Holocaust for more than six years, but his biggest achievements in the project came in the early phases when he commanded an army of hundreds of international accountants in an examination of millions of Swiss bank records. Volcker's investigation riveted further attention to increasing assertions of a despicable and profitable relationship between the Swiss and the Nazis and helped force the banks to agree to a settlement of $1.25 billion for the benefit of Holocaust survivors and their families.

As chairman of a joint committee representing Jewish groups and the Swiss banks, Volcker found himself in a strange, bare-knuckles world of rancorous verbal combat unlike anything he had known at the Fed or even in the most contentious corporate boardrooms. Volcker had to constantly force compromise from the two warring sides. The first meeting of the committee in his office in New York erupted in acrimony over the scope of the investigation.[35] The Jewish members stood up and threatened to walk out. At one point, Edgar Bronfman, the president of the World Jewish Congress but not formally a member of the committee, snapped at Volcker: "Who made you God? You're not chairman of the Fed now!"[36] The Jewish groups wanted more disclosure; the Swiss bank representatives wanted the appearance of a full investigation, but they volunteered considerably less than full cooperation. "There was a feeling of failed justice on the Jewish side," Volcker says. "And on the Swiss side, a feeling of unfair criticism. I think I was genuinely neutral."[37]

Amazing as it may seem with such a deeply emotional issue, Volcker truly was one of those uncommon people who could attack the problem with detachment. All his life he had operated in that mechanical way, intensely intellectual yet warm with friends, but piercingly to the point on the big issues, the business at hand.

He was Mr. Incorruptible. He never went looking for work; the work always came to him. And he was almost always reluctant to take it. It was a month before he finally said yes to the Jewish groups and the Swiss, who both nominated him as the referee in their battle royal. He was approached first by Israel Singer, the secretary general of the World Jewish Congress,[38] then by Edgar Bronfman Sr., the heir to the Seagrams fortune and the president of the World Jewish Congress.[39] Others from both sides appealed to him to step in. Finally, his old friend Fritz Leutwiler, whom he had gotten to know as chairman of the Swiss central bank and who had been a fellow board member of one of Switzerland's biggest companies, the Nestlé Corporation, tipped the balance. Volcker had not missed the social magnitude of an investigation into the role of the Swiss banks in the Holocaust, but in the end it was the personal connection that won him over. "Paul will do that for somebody he respects," says Michael Bradfield.[40] "That's Volcker."

CHAPTER THREE

THE POWER OF THE FED

Congress established the Federal Reserve Board in 1913 as an independent, self-financing body. The Fed, as it was widely known, was nominally responsible to Congress. But saddled with the difficult job of keeping the economy from either overheating with vaulting inflation or sagging into recession, it was inherently controversial. Despite its best efforts, recessions inevitably capped periods of prosperity and, in good times, prices often threatened to run away with the show—at which point the Fed would step in and apply the brakes. So, in practice, Congress preferred to keep its distance. If there was any heat to be taken, let the Fed take it. But, in fairness, on those rare occasions when the public was feeling good about the Fed—when it was even visible to the public—Congress was willing to forsake any claim on those brief moments of gratitude.

When Jimmy Carter was sworn in as the 39th president of the United States in 1976, Paul Volcker was running the Federal Reserve bank in New York, and that made him one of the most influential players in American finance. The New York bank conducted the trading in government securities that attempted to keep the American economy flowing evenly. It was the window for investors in other countries who bought and sold United States securities and it was America's center for transactions in the $1.6 trillion market in world currencies, the place where the pulse—and, more important, the worth—of the ever fluctuating dollar was tracked minute by minute. Volcker's bank was the operational arm of the Federal Reserve System—the nation's central bank, with a dozen member banks scattered around the country and headquartered in a grand marble palace in Washington, DC.

At the time, Arthur F. Burns was the chairman of the Federal Reserve Board. Imperious and often caustic, the pipe-smoking former professor of economics at Columbia University delighted in lecturing Congress, the public, and presidents of the United States. A stocky, energetic, and supremely self-confident man, Burns presided over the entire Federal Reserve System that comprised the Board of Governors in Washington and the 12 district banks and their outlying branches. By law and by virtue of personality, performance, and friendship, Volcker was Burns's right-hand man. Burns had worked closely with Volcker when Volcker was a high-ranking official in the Treasury Department, and ensured that he got the prestigious New York job in the summer of 1975.

For the White House, the Fed was personified by its chairman. Certainly, by all indications, when Carter thought of the Federal Reserve, he thought of Burns, and often not fondly. For Carter, who had managed to get through the

United States Naval Academy with only a single course even vaguely related to economics (personal finance),[1] the inner workings of the Federal Reserve were obscure, as they had been to most presidents. Volcker might have been a critically important part of national finance and economics, but, ensconced in his own stone palace in New York, a much more massive edifice than the Washington headquarters, he was well off Jimmy Carter's radar screen.

From the earliest days of the Federal Reserve, the New York bank has been the preeminent member bank, due in no small part to the bank's location in the heart of Wall Street. Its special trading functions put it at the center of national and international finance, and the power of the bank automatically accrued to its president. Despite the bank's prestige, it was not impossible for its president to lose clout. Volcker's predecessor, Alfred J. Hayes, managed to do that, but Volcker came in strong and stayed strong.

Of the heads of the 12 Federal Reserve banks, the president of the New York bank is the only permanent member of the Federal Open Market Committee (FOMC). The group takes its name from its mission of managing the tides of the economy through the sale of government securities in the open market. The committee is made up of the chairman and the six other members of the Federal Reserve Board in Washington, the president of the New York bank, and, in annual rotation, the presidents of 4 of the 11 other Federal Reserve banks around the country.

The committee tries to stimulate or cool the economy by raising or lowering the federal funds rate—the interest rate that banks charge each other for loans, and the main guidepost for interest rates in America. In his capacity as president, Volcker and his New York bank served as the committee's agent, selling securities in order to take money off the streets and slow the economy or buying in order to inject money into the system and give the economy a lift. In Fed talk, reducing the money in the system is known as *tightening;* increasing it is referred to as *easing.* The transactions are conducted throughout the day by a unit of the New York bank known mundanely as the Federal Open Market Committee Desk in a continuous exercise to keep the Fed funds rate where the committee decides it should be. These days the Desk employs about 50 men and women and trades billions of dollars in securities a week.

The New York bank, a 14-story fortress of gray Florentine marble with heavy wrought iron grills on its windows, occupies an entire block in the Wall Street district, near the New York Stock Exchange and some of the nation's largest banks and investment houses. As president, Volcker was not just a permanent member of the Federal Open Market Committee, but was also the vice chairman of the group. At committee meetings in Washington, he sat just to the right of the Fed chairman at the head of a long, graciously bowed mahogany table, looking out at the six other governors, as the members of the board are called, and at the presidents of the other Federal Reserve banks. All of the bank presidents attend committee meetings and participate in the discussions, even though only five, including the New York Fed president, have voting rights.

—

By the time Volcker had become president of the New York Fed that summer in 1975, he was well known among bankers and economists around the world. For five years, he had been the third-highest-ranking official in the Treasury Department. As undersecretary for monetary affairs, Volcker had devised a strategy in the early 1970s for breaking the linkage of the dollar to gold, and he was the United States' point man in negotiating new, lower price levels for the dollar against the currencies of the other major countries. The other countries did not welcome the devaluing of the dollar. They liked a strong dollar because it made the products they exported to the United States cheaper for American buyers; their sales were strong when the dollar was strong, weaker when the dollar became weaker.

It was tough for Volcker to get the other countries to come around to the United States' way of thinking. In one sense there was really no alternative for the other countries. Since the United States' economy was the biggest in the world, the others ultimately had to find a way to adjust. But they did not have to do so quickly or without a lot of grumbling. As undersecretary, it fell to Volcker to smooth the transition, and, when the other countries began to bend, to get them to bend a little more. In the process, Volcker developed close relationships with the princes of public finance around the world, not only the heads of the central banks and the finance ministers but also junior staffers who would later rise to positions of authority. Volcker worked closely with Helmut Schmidt of Germany and Valéry Giscard d'Estaing of France when they were finance ministers of their countries, and he stayed in touch as they rose to the top of their governments. Edward George was rather junior when he met Volcker and marveled at how the gangly American in the baggy suit commanded a room during the currency negotiations in the early 1970s.[2] He stayed in touch with Volcker, too, even as he rose to become governor of the Bank of England and became known as Sir Eddy.

—

Volcker moved into the huge wood-paneled presidential suite on the 10th floor of the Federal Reserve bank in New York on August 1, 1975, as Carter was heading into the stretch of his campaign for the White House. Volcker was a giant, both professionally and literally, striding back into familiar territory. At Princeton, he had written his undergraduate thesis on the Federal Reserve system. When he graduated summa cum laude in early 1949 and was on his way to graduate study at Harvard, a friend of his father's put in a good word for him at the New York Fed, and he worked there for several months as a research assistant. After getting a master's degree in political economy at Harvard and spending a year at the London School of Economics, Volcker became a staff economist at the New York Fed. He was there five years when David Rockefeller's Chase Bank lured him away. Now, on his first day as president of the New York bank, he made a small but important discovery: His legs would not fit under the elegantly carved mahogany desk that had been used by his five predecessors in the premier post outside Washington of one of the youngest but most powerful of the nation's institutions. Instead of wasting government money and ordering new furniture befitting the chief of the bank, Volcker turned to Anne Poniatowski for help. He had known her since his first job at the Fed in his student days and she had moved up the ladder to become an administrative assistant to the president and other senior New York Fed officials. Poniatowski could handle a simple thing like having a giant in the house. She called for the carpenters. They set to work fitting blocks to the base of the desk and soon Volcker had more than enough legroom.[3] The raising of the desk not only preserved a tradition, but was an example of the Puritan ethic that permeated Volcker and informed some of his most important decisions as president of the New York Fed, and later as chairman of the Federal Reserve System.

—

Volcker had not campaigned for the New York job, taking pride in the fact of never having sought any job after applying for his first full-time work as a staff economist at the New York Fed. Opportunity seemed always to come to him.

In 1957, John D. Wilson, a five-year veteran of the Fed himself and now the chief of research at the Chase Bank, invited Volcker to join him at Chase. Volcker did not have a career plan. He certainly was not committed to a lifetime at the Fed and he was eager to see what it was like to work in the private sector. For all its intellectual intensity, Volcker says, "the Fed was a pretty stuffy, bureaucratic place." Going to Chase "was a chance to see the world outside."[4]

Once Volcker was at Chase, David Rockefeller, the chairman of the bank, recruited him as his special assistant on a congressional commission on money and credit in America and for help, later, on an advisory commission to the Treasury Department, giving Volcker his first taste of official Washington. Rockefeller had felt immediately drawn to Volcker, and it would be the beginning of a lifelong relationship. "He just thought very clearly and expressed himself very clearly," Rockefeller says.[5] It was while Volcker was at

Chase that he was first tapped for a government job in Washington. Robert V. Roosa, a mentor to Volcker at the New York Fed, had moved to Washington to become undersecretary of the Treasury for monetary affairs in the early days of the Kennedy administration in 1961. The next year, Roosa brought Volcker to Washington as director of the Office of Financial Analysis to do long-term planning in the Treasury Department, then headed by C. Douglas Dillon.[6] Volcker quickly attracted the attention of Dillon, who added speechwriting to his duties and eventually promoted him to deputy undersecretary.[7] In 1965 Volcker returned to Chase to work again as an aide to Rockefeller, this time as a vice president dealing with international business. Then, as Richard Nixon was moving into the White House for his first term in 1969, Volcker got the call from Washington. Even though Volcker was a Democrat, he was asked to assume the third-highest job in the Treasury Department.

Volcker's work as undersecretary of the Treasury for monetary affairs would put him at the center of one of the revolutionary changes in international finance, the dissolution of the Bretton Woods agreement, named after the New Hampshire town in which it was reached. Under the Bretton Woods agreement, a fixed exchange rate for the world's currencies was established based on gold. The value of the dollar was set at $35 to an ounce of gold. All other currencies were pegged to the dollar. Under the Bretton Woods system, other countries could present dollars to the United States and receive gold. But, over the years, through the Marshall Plan and other generous aid programs and heavy spending on United States troops abroad, particularly in Germany and South Korea, great quantities of dollars accumulated in central bank vaults overseas. By the summer of 1971, other countries held three times more dollars than the United States held in gold, which meant that if everyone decided to cash in these dollars, the United States would eventually default.

Facing a crisis with demand for gold increasing, the United States abruptly announced it was breaking the deal. It would no longer exchange gold for dollars at a fixed rate. Instead, the dollar and other currencies would be allowed to float and find their own levels of value. It was a momentous development that infuriated America's trading partners and, for the first few days of its enactment, sent the world's currency markets into paroxysms. President Nixon announced the change and John B. Connolly, his flamboyant Treasury secretary, took center stage in explaining the decision. But Volcker was the architect of the move and he spent the next two years negotiating agreements with other countries.

It was an exciting and important job, and one that would help to create or solidify professional relationships that would serve Volcker well over the years. Volcker was now face to face with the most influential money people in the world. Often, to them, he was the United States. He may have been only an undersecretary, but he was held in high regard, and was even flown occasionally in his own Air Force plane. Once, when an official from another country challenged Volcker's presence in a room filled with more senior representatives, Valéry Giscard d'Estaing, then the French finance minister, jumped to the American's defense. "He is a minister," d'Estaing declared, instantly promoting Volcker and ending the matter.[8]

Throughout his career in government service Volcker

felt a tension between the excitement and satisfaction of serving the nation and financial responsibility toward his family. He never hungered for luxuries or great wealth, but he worried about earning enough to keep up with the medical costs of an ailing wife and a handicapped son, paying for the education of his son and daughter, and putting a little away in case he were suddenly struck down. "If I got hit by a bus," he asked rhetorically in a conversation with me in 2003, "what would have happened to them?"[9] His family, he said, in an interview as chairman of the Fed, were "the ones who'll pay for my indulgence in pursuing a career in public service."[10]

Volcker had taken a substantial pay cut when he left Chase for Washington and in 1973, after just four years at Treasury, the old concerns began to gnaw at him again. Perhaps it was time to take a job at a bank or one of the big brokerage houses in New York, where he could easily earn three or four times the $40,000 or so that the Treasury was paying.

Volcker's commitment to government service was gravely shaken by the disclosures of President Nixon's abuse of power in the Watergate scandal that came to light in the summer of 1972 as a result of a bungled burglary of Democratic party headquarters in Washington. "That was a big factor," Volcker says. "I remember thinking when Watergate first broke, 'What am I doing working for this guy? I ought to resign.'"[11]

Yet government service had a powerful pull. Volcker was in the midst of the international negotiations over the dollar and he decided not to leave, at least not just yet. But in early 1974, with his work on the dollar behind him and the ugliness of Watergate deepening around Nixon, Volcker felt restless and weary. There was plenty of important work to be done at Treasury, but it had somehow lost its edge for Volcker. "I'd done what I could," he says, "It was time to go."

Volcker says that in his early days in government he also chafed at constraints on his ability to fully speak his mind. He imagined more personal freedom as a private executive, though there were few examples of corporate leaders actually taking a stand on public policy. Years later, as chairman of the Fed, Volcker would rise above the bureaucracy and become a crusader against inflation, tax cuts, and budget deficits.

Overlaying all the other factors leading up to Volcker's departure from government in 1974 may have been a certain disappointment in never having been elevated to the top job, secretary of the Treasury. Even though Volcker had worked closely with secretary of the Treasury, John B. Connolly, on some of the most important economic projects in the government, when Connolly abruptly left in the spring of 1972, the post of secretary went to George P. Shultz, who was then Nixon's director of the budget. In 1973, Shultz brought in William E. Simon, a former Wall Street executive, to become deputy secretary of the Treasury, a notch above Volcker. It was at about that time that Volcker started seriously thinking about leaving the Treasury. Simon, who developed a close working relationship with Shultz, served simultaneously at Treasury and as Nixon's chief on energy policy and was known as the "energy czar." Shultz resigned in March 1974 and, a month later, Nixon appointed Simon secretary of the Treasury.[12]

Volcker submitted his resignation shortly before the Simon announcement.[13] But whether that was because

Simon was about to get the top job is not clear. He does seem to have acted abruptly; he had no job lined up and no definite plans. Yet years later, he insists "there was no one thing on the road to Damascus"[14] that forced his decision.

Volcker sometimes seems wistful, talking about the idea of his ever being secretary of the Treasury. "When you became secretary of the Treasury," he says, "obviously you got some glory. But then you get involved in all this political stuff. You've got to deal with Nixon trying to corrupt the IRS. You've got to go out campaigning for Republicans. I wasn't even a Republican. You had to deal with the operating side of the Treasury. You had to deal with a lot of political or semipolitical stuff, which is not my particular cup of tea."[15]

Having left the Treasury, Volcker, without a job in hand, was expecting to go to work on Wall Street. He'd been approached about private banking jobs many times while at the Treasury and assumed he would soon be employed, but with much higher pay and possibly less demanding hours.

—

Fed chairman Arthur Burns had other plans for Volcker. For five years, Volcker and Burns had been the nation's principal officials dealing with monetary policy. As chairman of the Fed, Burns was by far the more powerful of the two. On policy matters Volcker, as undersecretary, deferred to the secretary of the Treasury and, of course, the White House. But in practice, the Treasury secretaries relied on Volcker's expertise. Volcker mastered the intricacies of interest rates and foreign exchange rates, the essence of monetary policy. He took it as his duty to manipulate the two in what he regarded as the best interests of the United States. The Treasury secretaries were not always great financial technicians. But they were always out front, always the face of the department, weighing decisions on political merit as much as anything else, selling the administration's economic programs. Volcker was the chef, sifting the ingredients, blending them into a workman's stew. The Treasury secretaries were the president's dining room managers, usually taking the bows or the brickbats, sometimes giving a nod to the kitchen.

During Volcker's years at the highest levels of Treasury, he and Burns and a small group of other officials from the Treasury and the Fed met over lunch twice a week. On Mondays, they would be guests of the secretary of the Treasury at the Treasury's granite building adjacent to the White House. On Wednesdays, Volcker and two or three Treasury aides would walk a few blocks over to the Fed, past the great lawn of the Ellipse, past the headquarters of the Organization of American States and, finally, just before reaching the Fed on Constitution Avenue, past the chunky beige stone home of the Department of the Interior. As proud as the Fed was of its independence from the rest of government, the Fed chairman and the secretary of the Treasury recognized a common goal in keeping the economy vibrant. Whether they agreed precisely on how to do that or not, they knew they should at least be up to date on each other's thinking.

Volcker and Burns, in particular, had some fundamental disagreements. Volcker thought Burns should have kept a tighter rein on inflation, which would have made life more difficult for the White House, and Burns contended, unsuccessfully, that the United States in 1971 could have addressed its worsening balance of payments problem by persuading other major countries to incrementally raise the value of their currencies and effectively reduce the value of the dollar. But Treasury Secretary John Connolly and President Nixon adopted Volcker's logic: There was no way other countries would voluntarily act against their national interest. It was going to take brute force. After all, increasing the value of their currencies would make products of those countries more expensive for Americans. Sales of imported goods in the United States could therefore decline, hurting the manufacturers of everything from Japanese cars to French perfume and weakening the trade balances of the other countries. Volcker and Burns were definitely not cut from the same cloth, but both displayed commanding styles that, at least to those around them, suggested great self-confidence. They respected each other, and despite Volcker's direct, no-frills manner and Burn's ingrained pomposity and blustering, they somehow got along well.

As chairman, Arthur Burns was a kingmaker in the Federal Reserve System. When there were openings at any of the 12 Federal Reserve banks, he had the last word on who would fill them. Sometimes he made a point of having the first word as well.[16] In 1974, his choice to run the bank in New York was Volcker. "I wanted someone who was an expert in the monetary and banking area—a man of good character," Burns said.[17] "I wanted someone whom I knew personally and therefore I could trust. In my own mind, there were no competitors."

Volcker resisted. "It was time for me to be in the private sector," he says. "I'd been in the government most of my life. To some degree, I thought it was about time to make some money."[18]

It was also true that the New York job did not seem as exciting and challenging as making economic policy in Washington and flying around the world lining up international support. But Burns persisted. "He came and talked repeatedly about how he thought this would be a good thing for me," Volcker says. "He thought it would be a good thing for the Federal Reserve, but of course it would be a good thing for me.'"

Burns knew just how to reach Volcker's soft spot. "This is something you ought to do," Volcker recalls Burns saying.[19] "You're a public servant." In the end, Volcker agreed. But Burns and Volcker had a problem: There was no opening in New York. Alfred J. Hayes, a man of great reserve and formal bearing, had been president of the New York bank since taking over from Allen Sproul in 1956. By 1974 he had run the New York Fed for 18 years, far longer than anyone else. People who were involved with the Fed at that time say that Burns increasingly found Hayes to be irritating. Hayes preferred compromise to combat. "He was not inclined to rock the boat," says Peter D. Sternlight, an economist who spent 40 years at the New York Fed and knew both men well.[20] Sometimes at meetings, Hayes relied on notes, suggesting to some colleagues a lack of certainty and self-confidence. Boldness was not one of Hayes' traits, and, for a bulldozer like Burns, that may have been unsettling. Although nothing about Burns's discontent found its way into the newspapers at the time, Burns wanted Volcker sitting next to him at the Federal Open Market Committee meetings and he wanted him there right away. Quietly, Burns tried to persuade Hayes to step down before reaching the mandatory retirement age of 65 on July 4, 1975. Hayes, of course, knew he did not have to go early and, on that issue, at least, he would not budge.

By the time Burns began promoting the New York position, Volcker had left Treasury and had no job. Now, with Hayes insisting on staying on in New York, Volcker needed a place to bide his time and draw a paycheck. That spring Volcker had given a speech at Princeton. He had spoken with the dean of the Woodrow Wilson School of Public and International Affairs at that time and the dean wondered whether Volcker might like to return to his alma mater as a senior fellow. That now seemed like a splendid idea. So for the next academic year, Volcker cooled his heels amidst the bucolic environs of Princeton. His main duty was to conduct a graduate seminar in international finance, something he could easily accomplish. So, when Hayes was finally ready to go, shortly after his 65th birthday, Volcker was ready to step in.

Burns now had his handpicked man in New York and at his side in the most important Federal Reserve meetings in Washington. But much sooner than he had ever expected, Burns's partnership with Volcker, as well as his dreams of greater national influence, would come to an end.

CHAPTER FOUR

CHAIRMAN

Just two-and-a-half years after he installed Volcker at the New York Fed, Burns was gone.

Appointed chairman by President Richard M. Nixon in January 1970, Burns had loved his time at the Fed. He had coached Nixon on economics during the 1968 presidential campaign, and, with Nixon in the White House, Burns made his desire for the chairman's post clear. Robert Solomon, an economist at the Federal Reserve Board at the time, recalls that Nixon asked William McChesney Martin Jr., one of the most highly regarded chairmen in the history of the Fed, to step aside.[1] Martin had done nothing to warrant early departure, but Nixon held him partly responsible for his defeat in the 1960 presidential elections. Martin had refused to lower interest rates to jump-start the economy and produce a rosier picture for the incumbent Republican administration. Martin rejected Nixon's request to retire early, just as Hayes later would rebuff Burns. During the end of Martin's term, Burns served as an economic adviser in the White House waiting for Martin to move on. Once ensconced as chairman, Burns found that the Fed became a wonderful platform, ideally suited for his personality. He was neither understated nor self-effacing. "He liked the idea of having a powerful, influential position," says Peter D. Sternlight, an economist who spent most of his professional life working at the Federal Reserve bank in New York and at the Treasury Department in Washington.[2]

As the end of his second term as chairman approached in late 1977, Burns made clear to the administration that he wanted to be reappointed for another four years. That was a decision now in the hands of President Jimmy Carter. But, according to press reports at that time, Carter did not appreciate Burns's abrasive and superior manner. Burns's bid ended with a stunning phone call from Carter: Burns's life at the Fed suddenly was over. The president would appoint G. William Miller, chief executive of the Textron Corporation, as the new chairman.

Miller was known in the corporate world as tough, hard-driving, and confident and had served on the nine-member board of the Federal Reserve bank in Boston. However, he was not an economist and he had no expertise in monetary policy, which was the main business of the Fed. The Boston board and those of the other regional banks maintained a passive, supportive relationship with the president of their bank and the bank's technical staffs. The board members kept the Fed up to date with the thinking in the business community, but they had little influence on policy.[3]

Miller's lack of the experience and skills most needed at the Fed made him suspect to some of the bank's most important constituencies: Wall Street and the professional economists of America, not to mention the men and women who had devoted their lives to the inner workings of the Fed. None were ever fans of Miller as chairman, and they became less enamored with him as time went on. Part of the problem was that Miller brought his harsh corporate style to the Fed. He was known to place a three-minute egg timer on the table at board meetings to limit the often rambling discourse, and worse, he tried to ban smoking. But the members of the Federal Reserve Board, seasoned economists serving virtually irrevocable 14-year appointments, were used to doing things their way. At his first board meeting, Miller brought along a small sign: "Thank you for not smoking." Within minutes, the governors were filling the room with smoke as usual.

As Wall Street and the economic pros saw it, Miller never behaved like a Fed chairman. He not only spoke clearly and to the point—violating the historic commitment of chairmen to obfuscation—but in June 1978, a few months after taking charge, he aligned himself with the minority in a vote of the Federal Reserve Board, something almost unheard of for a chairman. Ending up in the minority raised questions about leadership. "He lost status in the market and in the Fed itself," says Stephen H. Axilrod, a senior staff official at the Fed for more than 30 years. "The vote as much as said to the market, 'If I'm listening to the chairman, I'm not necessarily listening to the person in charge.'"[4] Moreover, the majority had moved to raise the discount rate—the interest rate that the Fed charges banks for loans—signaling a tightening of money. Miller's opposition suggested that he might be more interested in serving the needs of the White House than those of the economy. This, in turn, raised questions about Miller's adherence to the tradition of the political independence of the Fed and its chairman.

More than anything, for professional economists, Miller's vote demonstrated that he was out of his depth. "You have to have some sense of what the board members are thinking," Axilrod says. "Miller was new. He didn't have any real sense of his board. He should have sensed the direction and postponed the vote. Or he could have voted with the majority. It was considered bad judgment."[5]

There was more bad news for Miller in his future. In April of 1979, just a day before the Federal Open Market Committee (FOMC) was to meet for one of its discussions on whether to raise rates or take any other action, Miller gave the press a preview of how he saw the secret session unfolding. In several interviews that day, he proclaimed that he saw no need to raise interest rates.[6] Miller was counterpunching in an intramural dust-up with Secretary of the Treasury W. Michael Blumenthal, who had been pushing publicly and privately among Carter's economic advisers for an increase in interest rates. Even so, Miller's remarks, on the eve of a meeting, were considered by those inside and outside the Fed as an ill-mannered preemption of the committee's authority.

—

For years, inflation had been eroding wealth in America. By 1978, when Miller arrived at the Fed, inflation was the number one economic problem. As chairman, Miller argued for gradualism. Like Burns and some other board members, he worried that by sharply increasing interest rates—the standard medicine for inflation—the Fed would push the economy into a recession.

His approach did not alleviate the problem, and through most of 1979 the economic picture grew worse, due in large part to a growing fuel crisis. Because of the revolution that led to the fall of the Shah of Iran, oil exports to the United States from Iran had slowed. A fuel shortage developed in the United States, resulting in long lines at gas stations that sometimes erupted into violence. By midyear, the cost of gas and oil shipments to the United States from the Organization of Petroleum Exporting Countries had jumped 60 percent.[7] Increased fuel costs were slowing the economy and many economists, including those at Miller's Fed, were expecting a recession. Unemployment and inflation were rising. By June 1979, inflation was running at an annual rate of 13 percent. At the same time, the value of the dollar had been declining against other major currencies.

For months, Treasury Secretary Blumenthal had been urging Miller to raise interest rates to counter inflation and bolster the dollar. He had also been agitating for support among the economic advisers in the White House. Miller was reluctant to move, concerned that higher interest rates would deepen a recession and also fail to halt inflation. If the recession was mild and brief, Miller reasoned, lower rather than higher interest rates could contribute to a rise in productivity that could dampen inflation. In a few months, President Carter would be mounting a campaign for reelection and liked Miller's restrained approach. In the spring, in a speech in Dallas, Blumenthal went public with his argument for higher interest rates. (It was that speech that prompted Miller to call in news reporters just before the FOMC meeting in April.) Miller complained to President Carter about the pressure from Blumenthal and the president told Blumenthal and the economic advisers in the White House to back off.

By early July, the Carter presidency was in grave trouble. Carter had promised a more prosperous and decent America and now, two-and-a-half years into his presidency, he seemed to have lost touch with the people. Though still regarded as a man of high moral principles, he seemed weak, indecisive, and ineffectual, regarded more as a manager than a leader—and the frustrating lines at the gas stations called even his managerial ability into question. Tully Plesser, a political analyst and pollster with the Republican National Committee, classified Carter as a "well-intentioned amateur."[8]

Shortly after flying back to Washington from a conference in Tokyo on the international oil crisis, Carter decided to address the nation on July 5, 1979. He spent much of the Fourth of July at Camp David, the Presidential retreat in the Catoctin mountains of Maryland, working on the speech. Late in the day he canceled the talk and decided not to return to the White House.

Instead, he remained in seclusion at Camp David and began 10 days of long, rambling conversations with select groups that he hoped would help him get back in touch with the nation. One day he heard from businessmen, university presidents, labor leaders, and the president of the Audubon Society. Another day it was clergy and civil rights leaders, oil executives, and oil industry consultants. He met with members of congress, governors of states, and mayors. He then left Camp David to visit ordinary families in Pennsylvania. Mostly, President Carter listened and took notes.

On Sunday, July 15, Carter settled at his desk in the Oval Office at 10:00 P.M. and spoke to the American people. He reported on the discussions at Camp David, outlined a half dozen steps for reducing dependence on foreign oil, and told Americans that working together to solve the energy problem could bring new vigor to the country.[9]

But the speech began on a somber note. "The true problems of our nation are much deeper . . . than gasoline lines or energy shortages, deeper even than inflation or recession," Carter said. He conceded that he had had "just mixed success" as president and said that, partly as a result of the conversations at Camp David, he sensed that a deep discontent had been building since the assassinations of John F. Kennedy and Martin Luther King Jr., and as America struggled through the agony of Vietnam and the shock of Watergate and then watched inflation eat away at family savings and the value of the dollar abroad. The country, Carter said, was in the midst of "a crisis of confidence." He spoke of "a growing doubt about the meaning of our lives," and of "a loss of a unity of purpose for our nation." The situation was critical. "The erosion of our confidence in the future," Carter said, "is threatening to destroy the social and the political fabric of America."[10]

Carter's specific proposals helped him look more decisive to some Americans, but the lasting impression was of a country in trouble. Clark Clifford, a Washington lawyer, former Defense secretary, and Democratic Party sage, said Carter told him and other visitors to Camp David that "he had a feeling that the country was in a mood of widespread national malaise."[11] During the talks at Camp David, William Safire suggested in one of his columns for *The New York Times* that the president would "try to transfer the wide dissatisfaction with his own performance into a 'national malaise.'"[12] Though Carter never used the word *malaise* in his address, it nevertheless became known as his "malaise speech."

In the Sunday night address, Carter quoted one of his visitors to Camp David as saying, "Some of your Cabinet members don't seem loyal. There is not enough discipline among your disciples."[13] Back in Washington, on Tuesday, Carter suggested to his cabinet and senior staff members that they offer their resignations. All 34 of them did so immediately. The mass resignation startled the country and the world. The reaction was strongest in countries with parliamentary governments, which interpreted the resignations as a protest rather than an act of compliance. Because of international concern that the Carter government would fall, the value of the dollar plunged and the price of gold reached a record high of $300 an ounce.[14]

On Thursday, two days after the resignations, the White House announced news that would create another uproar: the dismissals of Joseph Califano, the secretary of Health, Education and Welfare, and W. Michael Blumenthal, the secretary of the Treasury. The removal of three more cabinet officials soon followed; the other cabinet members stayed on.

Both Califano and Blumenthal were highly regarded by experts in their fields and good at their jobs. But they had run afoul of Hamilton Jordan, the president's chief of staff; Jody Powell, the president's press secretary; and other Georgians that Jimmy Carter had brought into his inner circle in the

White House. The administration regarded the two cabinet officials as too independent, too outspoken, and perhaps disloyal. From the outside it looked like Jimmy Carter was sacrificing competence to style, inciting further criticism.

Carter had already lined up Patricia Roberts Harris, the secretary of Housing and Urban Development, to replace Califano, but he spent much of that Thursday scrambling to find someone willing to become secretary of the Treasury before telling Blumenthal he was through.

Carter first turned to David Rockefeller, the chairman of Chase Manhattan Bank. When Rockefeller declined, Carter approached A. W. Clausen, the chairman of the Bank of America. Clausen also said no. Finally Carter contacted Miller, who was in San Francisco making a speech. While finance professionals had criticized Miller, the head of the supposedly apolitical Federal Reserve, as being too sensitive to the needs of the White House and too much of a team player, the Carter administration saw those qualities as virtues. When Carter asked Miller to take charge of Treasury, he did not hesitate.

Now Carter had an opening at the Fed.

—

In New York, Volcker learned about the upheaval almost immediately, and his first reaction was that he was not in the running for the job. While Volcker was more than qualified to be chairman, he thought he lacked crucial connections. "I didn't have the qualification of knowing the president," he says. "I didn't have the qualification of being particularly close to Miller or anyone else in the administration."[15]

Volcker thought his real opportunity to become chairman

was in early 1978, when Carter decided not to reappoint Arthur Burns. "I was fresher from Washington," he says. "It was obvious that I could have been a logical candidate."[16] Aides to Carter agreed. Volcker had, indeed, been on a list of potential chairmen then. But this time around, in moments of pessimism, Volcker would tell himself to forget it, that no president of the New York Fed, for all its power and influence, had ever been called to Washington as chairman. In brighter moments, he might concede: "Well, I had a shot at it. But, I wasn't sitting there waiting for the telephone to ring." "At that time," Volcker says, "I was making up my mind on whether or not I wanted to go private. Before I went to the New York bank I thought, well, okay, once I'm there five years, it's time to leave. And if I was thinking about anything, I was thinking about what kind of a job, when should I leave, when should I get a job in the private sector."[17]

Almost as soon as word reached Europe that Miller had left a vacancy at the Fed, central bankers there began telling news reporters that Volcker would be a natural choice.[18] But Carter's instinct was to go back to Rockefeller and Clausen. Again, they both said no. In his memoir, David Rockefeller said he concluded he was not the right choice. "I would have been responsible for implementing a set of draconian policies to wring inflation from the economy and stabilize the dollar," he said. "As a wealthy Republican with a well-known name, and a banker to boot, it would have been extremely difficult for me to make the case for tight monetary policy and sell it to a skeptical Congress and an angry public."[19]

Newspapers and magazines reported that President Carter had also considered Robert V. Roosa,[20] Volcker's mentor at the Fed and Treasury and, at the time, a partner at the New York brokerage firm of Brown Brothers, Harriman. Carter sounded out Bruce MacLaury, whom Volcker had brought to Washington from the New York Fed to assist him at Treasury. MacLaury had gone on to become president of the Federal Reserve Bank in Minneapolis, and in the summer of 1979 became president of the Brookings Institution, the economics research center in Washington.

Though his name had been on the list of possible replacements for Burns, this time, Volcker was not in the picture.

—

Two days after Carter appointed Miller secretary of the Treasury, the president, according to author William Neikirk, telephoned Anthony Solomon, the undersecretary of the Treasury for monetary affairs, at his home in suburban Washington. The president said he hoped Solomon would stay on under Miller and asked who he thought would be good as chairman of the Fed. Solomon did not hesitate. "Paul Volcker," he said.[21]

To Solomon's surprise, the president replied: "Who's Paul Volcker?"

After Solomon, in Neikirk's telling of the episode, brought the president up to date on Volcker, Carter asked, "Why not David Rockefeller?"

Again, the answer was evident to Solomon. "Because," he said, "David doesn't have the technical understanding to conduct monetary policy and would, in my opinion, be murdered on the Hill [in Congress] when he appeared to testify before committees."[22]

With the Fed loaded with experts, Carter did not see why the chairman personally needed to know all that much about how the economy worked. "Unlike some other policy-making jobs," Solomon told Carter, "the chairman of the Federal Reserve must have the understanding of how the economy works and how monetary policy impacts on the economy. He must be able to preside over a very difficult decision-making process, and he must be able to articulate it very carefully because, more than any other single person, the markets are impacted by what he says."[23]

Carter surely had not missed the criticism of Miller, who lacked those very skills. But the lesson apparently had not sunk in. Even after hearing Solomon outline the qualities needed in a Fed chairman, Carter still thought David Rockefeller would make a good choice for the position and tried to get him to take the job. In turning the president down, Rockefeller recommended Volcker.[24]

After his initial failures at recruiting a new Fed chairman, Carter delegated the task to Vice President Walter Mondale, who in turn handed the job to his chief of staff Richard Moe. On Sunday, July 22, as author William Greider recounted the effort, Moe was in his office in the White House working the phones. As Moe searched for a new Fed chairman, one name came up again and again: Volcker.

"It was a very intense and compressed process, very rushed," Moe told Greider. "The big factor was: we've got to reassure the markets. That's all we heard. Coming in the wake of the Camp David meetings and the Cabinet changes, people were very nervous about the direction we were going. I wouldn't call it panic but there was clearly a level of concern. We've got a problem on our hands and we have to do it right."[25]

The only problem with Volcker, as Moe saw it, was concern that he might not be a team player. "Nobody ever questioned his intellectual credentials," Moe said. "People knew that he was a very conservative fellow. But that never dissuaded the president on appointments anyway. The only question was whether he could work with the White House the way Bill Miller had. Miller was very close to the White House on monetary policy. That's the way any White House wants it." What Moe had heard about Volcker was that "he's a very strong-willed, strong-minded person who may or may not be prepared to coordinate policy with you."[26]

Based on this, Moe told Carter that Volcker might not be his man.[27] Yet on Monday, William Miller telephoned Volcker in New York and told him the president would like to see him.[28]

The next day, Tuesday, July 24, Volcker went to the White House. His main concern, he said years later, was for Carter to understand the type of Fed chairman he would be.[29] The meeting ran about an hour. Carter told author Carl Biven that Volcker sprawled on a couch as they talked, adding, "I think he was smoking a cigar." Indeed, the president did not know much about his visitor. "I didn't really know whether Paul Volcker was a Democrat or a Republican," Carter told Biven.[30]

Volcker recalled doing most of the talking.[31] "I told him the Federal Reserve was going to have to be tighter and that it was very important that its independence be maintained,"

Volcker says.[32] Walking out of the White House, Volcker said to himself, "That's the end of that. He'll never offer me the job.[33]

Later that afternoon, Greider reports, Gerald Rafshoon, Carter's media coordinator, got a phone call from Bert Lance. Lance, an old banker friend from Georgia and Carter's budget director before he was forced to resign, had a message for the president.[34] "I don't know who the president is thinking of for Fed chairman," he said. "But I want you to tell him something for me. He should not appoint Paul Volcker. If he appoints Volcker, he will be mortgaging his reelection to the Federal Reserve."[35]

Rafshoon went to see Carter and passed on Lance's warning: The appointment of Volcker would mean higher interest rates and higher unemployment and the outcome of the 1980 election would be "mortgaged" to the Federal Reserve. Carter smiled and thanked Rafshoon, Greider reported.[36]

Volcker flew back to New York and that evening went to dinner with two old friends, Lawrence S. Ritter and Robert Kavesh. Ritter had worked with Volcker as a young staff member at the New York Fed and was chairman of the finance department at New York University's Stern School of Business. Kavesh had studied with Volcker in graduate school at Harvard and had also become a professor at the New York University business school. Volcker told them "with a certain sense of relief that, after my performance, I surely wouldn't be asked to pull up stakes to return to Washington and disrupt the family."[37]

The next morning the phone rang in Volcker's apartment. It was 7:30 A.M. and Volcker and his wife were still in bed.[38] President Carter was on the line. He wanted Volcker for the job.

—

Bankers, business leaders, and government officials in New York and Washington and around the world hailed the appointment. The stock and bond markets rallied and the dollar regained some of its losses. "He chose the right man, the best of all the possible choices," said Larry Wachtel, a stock analyst for the New York brokerage firm of Bache Halsey Stuart Shields.[39] "Seldom has President Carter used his appointive power so well," said Gabriel Hauge, the retired chairman of the Manufacturers Hanover Trust Company, one of the nation's largest banks.[40]

Volcker's appointment was good news to others outside of big business. The small savings banks scattered across America welcomed his nomination as well. "It puts to rest the rumor that we're not going to have an independent Fed chairman," said Raymond D. Campbell, the president of the Oberlin Savings Bank Co. in Oberlin, Ohio, with $41.3 million in deposits. Campbell was also the chairman of the trade group of the savings banks, the Independent Bankers Association of America.[41]

Stuart Eizenstat, President Carter's adviser on domestic policy, told William Greider that with the economy looking bleak and with the Carter administration in turmoil, the president and his staff concluded that they had no choice but to pick Volcker. "Volcker was selected because he was the candidate of Wall Street," Eizenstat said.[42] "This was their price, in effect. What was known about him? That he was able and bright. And it was also known that he was conservative. What wasn't known was that he was going to impose some very dramatic changes."

On the afternoon of July 25, Volcker called a press conference at the New York Fed and that evening at 9:00, during prime time, Carter, for the first time in his presidency, addressed the press in the ornate East Wing of the White House rather than in a drab auditorium in the Executive Office building. Carter fielded questions about the economy and his cabinet shake-up and elaborated on his announcement that morning of the Volcker appointment.

In their separate meetings with reporters, Volcker and Carter gave the first hint that they held strikingly different views of how to deal with the ailing economy. Inflation, they agreed, was a monster that had to be contained. They each spoke of stability, but they had different visions of what that meant. Carter told the reporters he wanted "to maintain our steady course and to dwell as best I can on a balanced growth in the economy." It was time, he said, "for stability," time "for continuation of our present economic monetary and budgetary policies."[43] Volcker spoke of *price* stability. To his way of thinking, the only way to get price stability was to drive up interest rates to the point where the economy stalled, to where people no longer wanted to buy. Then prices would begin falling and you would begin to see stability replace the upward climb of inflation. That was not Carter's definition of stability. Volcker's approach would not be a continuation of Miller's way, gradually raising interest rates. Volcker sent a blunt message: "Our job," he told the reporters, "is to maintain a steady, disciplined policy."[44] This was not a man preparing to temporize. As Volcker saw it, Americans had to understand that inflation was going to be crushed. Then, and only then, would they end the pattern of buying as much as they could today because they believed everything would cost more tomorrow. "If we are going to progress and prosper," he continued at his news conference, "we need a sense of confidence that we are moving toward price stability at home and a sense of strong confidence in the dollar internationally."[45] Both objectives translated into higher interest rates, finance professionals and economists knew. This was radically different from the moderate approach Carter was advocating.

Although Volcker was promoting a much tougher strategy than Carter's, many thought the president and his new Fed chairman were in harmony on the issue. In an editorial published the day after the announcement of Volcker's nomination, *The New York Times* said it was unlikely that the Fed, under new direction, would "make any sudden shifts." If there were changes, the *Times* said, "the changes will be largely symbolic."[46]

In his way, perhaps, Volcker was not trying to mislead. He made a point in his news conference of declaring that he did not want the president "to be under any illusion about what my views were."[47] That may have been true. After all, he was speaking just the way he always spoke. But, of course, that was in Fedspeak. Whether or not Jimmy Carter was later surprised to see the ferocity of Volcker's assault on inflation, there surely would have been no point for him in those early days to have suggested that he and his new appointee were on divergent courses. And, of course, the president could always have hoped that he might influence his appointee by spelling out his views on the best way to proceed.

A few days later, Volcker went up to Capitol Hill for his confirmation hearing before the Senate Banking Committee and its chairman, Senator William Proxmire, the Wisconsin Democrat. The hearing was going to be a cakewalk. On the day of the nomination, Proxmire had told reporters: "Paul Volcker is a man of great intellect and proven leadership ability."[48]

During the hearing, nearly all of Proxmire's Senate colleagues took time to praise Volcker for his experience and demonstrated capabilities. But they also pressed him on how harsh he expected to be in attempting to slay the dragon of inflation.[49] He was somewhat less forthcoming with the senators than in his press conference with financial reporters in New York. Perhaps the more formal circumstances and the theoretical possibility that the senators could contest his nomination led him to be more circumspect. In any case, by the time of the confirmation hearing, the chatter among finance professionals was that interest rates were almost certainly going to increase. The senators may well have understood which way Volcker was headed. Yet, perhaps more for the benefit of their constituents back home, they sought assurances that Volcker would somehow quell inflation without forcing more people out of work, without causing more economic distress.

Some of the questions sounded combative. Following custom, the chairman, Senator Proxmire, led off. "You may be the personification of Wall Street and international banking," he told Volcker. "You're viewed as a hard money, big business conservative. What's your answer to the fear that—in the immortal words of William Jennings Bryan—you may choose to 'crush down upon the brow of labor the crown of gold,' by pushing high interest rates to levels that would be punishing and create more unemployment and be very difficult for small business, the farmer and the working people?"[50]

Using much less vivid language, Volcker had already acknowledged in his conversation with the president in the Oval Office and in his press conference that the picture Proxmire was painting was close to what he had in mind. But now, in the Senate, he did not want to respond directly. He pointed out that the country was facing great problems and recalled that he had persistently spoken of the need for stability in terms of inflation and the value of the dollar abroad. "I don't want interest rates any higher than they have to be," he said, without giving any clue as to how high he thought they might ultimately have to rise and just how difficult life in America might become.

Proxmire tried again. He noted that Volcker had voted in favor of interest rate increases the previous March and April, in contrast to his predecessor Miller and the majority on the Federal Open Market Committee. "Does this mean we enter this recession with the likelihood of a tight monetary policy and possible interest rates at an even higher level?" the senator asked.

Volcker sidestepped the question, saying, "I don't think it would be appropriate for me to comment on what particular moves might be necessary or desirable in the near future."[51] Still, he said wryly, he did not think that there was evidence to suggest "that the economy is suffering grievously from a shortage of money."

To the economists listening, the answer was clear. Everyone knew the economy was in trouble. If there was no shortage of money, as indeed was the case, then perhaps there was an oversupply. And the remedy available to the Fed was to reduce that oversupply by tightening, jacking up interest rates.

Proxmire did not pursue the point. Well into the two-and-a-half-hour hearing, Senator Nancy Landon Kassebaum, Republican of Kansas, picked up on Volcker's facetious reference to the more than ample money supply, seeking an answer everyone could understand. "Does this mean that you do feel that interest rates should be higher?" she asked.

Volcker was just not going to say, one way or the other, however obvious the answer might be. He had been a Fed man too long. "I don't think I want to begin my career as chairman by projecting just where interest rates might be or where they should be," he said.[52]

"Thank you," Senator Kassebaum replied. She was not going to push Volcker either.

The senators may have known as well as Volcker that interest rates and inflation and the value of the dollar in international markets were intertwined. Yet several of the senators expended a good deal of energy that day in laying down a trail in the Congressional Record to show voters their lack of sympathy for any policy that favored a strong dollar and good international trade relations over concerns about inflation and unemployment at home—whether or not their comments had any economic logic.

One senator taking that line, Donald W. Riegle, Jr., a Democrat from Michigan, worried that Volcker's focus would be more on international finance and "less toward domestic economic policy." The two issues were inseparable, Volcker said: "If we try to distinguish them, we get into trouble," adding, "I see them as part of one piece." In his questioning of Volcker, Riegle continued to juxtapose domestic and international economics, but his bottom line was a mutual prayer shared with his senate colleagues that day. It was his strongest hope, he said, "that we would not get fixed on a course where the belief was that the economy had to go through the wringer and that monetary policy would remain restrictive, and we would endure an overly severe and overly long recession."[53]

On August 6, at the swearing-in ceremony for Volcker as the new chairman of the Fed and G. William Miller as the new secretary of the Treasury, in the glittering East Room of the White House, President Carter again delivered his steady-as-you-go message. "Now," he said, "is not the time to change course."[54]

The newly installed chairman of the Federal Reserve Board was going to do what he knew to be right, no matter what. His years of study, his sense of civic duty, and his calm detachment from the heat of politics would guide him in his decisions. Indeed, all of Volcker's life up to now would come to bear on this moment and would have a profound effect on economic history.

CHAPTER FIVE

YOUTH

aul Volcker grew up in the shadow of New York, in the suburban town of Teaneck, New Jersey. From the kitchen window of the family home on Longfellow Avenue, he could the see the spire of the Empire State Building shimmering in the distance across the Hudson River, and in half an hour he could be in Times Square.

Yet as close as Teaneck was to the great city, it had the feel of an entirely different world. It was filled with trees and parks and quiet streets of modest Tudor and Dutch Colonial style houses and a fair share of ordinary clapboard and brick houses of no particular heritage. Teaneck High School looked like a crusader's castle and boasted its own football stadium and running track. The main shopping district consisted of a few blocks of restaurants and small shops and a movie theater along Cedar Lane. The overall impression was residential, verging on rural, nothing at all like the small, gritty city of Hackensack on the western edge of Teaneck, not even as commercially developed as Englewood to the east. "It was an idyllic place to grow up," says Dr. Donald W. Maloney, a classmate of Volcker's at Teaneck High School.[1]

In 1949, the United States Army Corps of Engineers looked at 10,000 communities in the United States and concluded that Teaneck was the very model of small-town America. The Army sent in a photographer and mounted an exhibit that, apparently without a moment of self-consciousness, was shipped off to Germany and Japan as an example of what those countries might strive for as they were rebuilding after World War II. Teaneck was the real home of Ozzie and Harriet Nelson before they began playing themselves in their radio and television series, from the mid-1940s to the mid-1960s, about a happy, middle-class American family.[2] Later, Pat Boone, a movie and television star who personified American wholesomeness, chose Teaneck as his home.

Volcker and his three older sisters moved to Teaneck with their parents shortly after their father, Paul A. Volcker Sr., was recruited as Teaneck's first town manager in late 1930. Paul Sr. was a natural for the job. The town manager form of government was just beginning to take hold in America, and he was one of the few people with experience in the new field. Five years earlier, the resort town of Cape May on the southern coast of New Jersey, in debt and disgusted with its leaders, had been the first community in the state to adopt town manager government. The senior Volcker, a civil engineer with a degree from Rensselaer Polytechnic Institute, had been working in Lebanon, Pennsylvania, first as the city engineer, then as manager of the chamber of commerce. Cape May hired him away.

When the Volckers arrived in Teaneck, near the beginning of the Depression, the town was close to bankruptcy. Paul's father saved money right away by agreeing to also serve as the town engineer for one extra dollar a year.[3] Then he went to work putting the town's finances in order.

Tall, stern, and more of a listener than a talker, Paul Volcker Sr. projected a sense of serious purpose and integrity, characteristics his son would exhibit decades later. "For years," he said in his retirement speech in 1950, "I have made it a point to speak as briefly and as concisely as possible."[4] During his time in public office he generally kept people at arm's length. But it was not a style he had to work at. At home, he was also distant and aloof. "Emotionally distant," his son, Paul Jr., says. "I mean, he was there. He paid attention. But he was not warm and cuddly."[5] With his wife, he was respectful and close, but they both came naturally to a reserved demeanor. "She had a hard time expressing love and devotion," Virginia Volcker Streitfeld, one of Paul's sisters, says of their mother.[6] "Some mothers will tell you, 'You're wonderful; I love you.' You knew she would always be there if there was ever a problem. You had a big sense of security. But there was not a lot of emotion." In a rare moment of public introspection, Paul Sr. admitted in his retirement speech that he suspected some people thought of him as "a cold fish."[7]

Much of the nature of his parents passed directly to Paul Volcker Jr. As chairman of the Federal Reserve, it served him well. A certain remove had become part of the public expectation of Federal Reserve chairmen, and it proved to be a useful approach in fending off questions from members of Congress and journalists.

Volcker's friends and colleagues say they rarely if ever recall his drifting off into tales of his early days or of his parents, as so many people do. Most of them never heard more than a word or two—at most—about his highly regarded father and his own youth. Ask Volcker a question about monetary policy and his response flowed clear and precise. But ask him to help set the scene on a particular day in his life, as I did in interviews for this book, and he would shake his head, his lips pursed in a half smile. "Trivial," he might say, by way of commentary, if he decided to say anything at all. He often seemed good-natured during our numerous meetings together, sometimes grumpy and irritable. But never a chatterbox. Some things that would roll off the tongues of most people just don't come up with him. He never mentioned to his daughter, Janice, for example, that the town green in Teaneck was named in honor of her grandfather. "Oh, my God!" she exclaimed when I told her. "I'll have to go by and see it." Until I mentioned it, he says, it never occurred to him that his wedding anniversary is on September 11, the day the World Trade Center was destroyed by terrorists in 2001. It didn't mean that he didn't love his wife or that the attack did not stun him; his mind just doesn't work that way.

Frugality was a family tradition. The Volcker girls made their own clothing,[8] and Paul Sr. wore double-breasted tweed suits until they frayed. Most days, Paul Sr. went home for lunch. He drove unpretentious, sensible cars, usually dark-colored Plymouths and DeSotos, often models with jump seats to accommodate a family of six with all but mother over six feet tall. Volcker displayed his frugality one day when I went with him after breakfast at his Manhattan apartment to a dry cleaner and shoe repair shop. He was trying to salvage a stained tie and was ordering yet another retread for an old, but certainly serviceable, pair of black cap-toed oxfords.

As the town manager, Volcker's father held the purse strings of Teaneck. He held them tight and was privately accorded the nickname "high-pockets." "When a person's got deep pockets, it generally means you can get into them," says Dick Rodda, who served for 40 years as Teaneck's director of parks and recreation. "When he's got high pockets, he doesn't want to give anything to anybody, including himself. He wanted results and he wanted them at low cost."[9]

Paul Adolph Volcker Jr. was born in Cape May on September 5, 1927, about two years after his father had become town manager. He was three years old when the new job took the family to Teaneck. Until his birth, there had been three Volcker children, all girls and all born while their father was working in Lebanon, Pennsylvania. A fourth sister, Eleanor, was born in Lebanon, but she contracted pneumonia and died at the age of four months.

Paul Jr. was the baby in a family of strong-willed sisters, born to a strong-willed Teutonic couple. At five or six, he slept in a little alcove, then moved to one of the rooms in the attic. It was only after his sisters had gone off on their own that he was given the front room. The family called Paul "Buddy" to distinguish him from his father.

The girls, Ruth, Louise, and Virginia, had witnessed the virtues of prudent, righteous behavior in their parents, and took it upon themselves to see that their little brother got the message. "We acted like three mothers," says Virginia Volcker Streitfeld, who is three years older than Paul and his only surviving sister. "We were mother hens, in a way, making sure he did the right thing."[10]

All the girls went to college and, far from typical in the 1940s, took up careers. Ruth, who was nearly 11 years older than Paul, earned a degree in library science at Simmons College in Boston and worked for Eastman Kodak in Rochester as a research librarian.[11] Toward the end of World War II, Kodak recruited her for the Manhattan Project, which developed the atomic bomb, and she was sent to work at a facility in Oakridge, Tennessee. After the Manhattan Project ended, Ruth moved to a Kodak chemical plant in Kingsport, Tennessee. She remained in Kingsport after retirement and died there in 1991 at age 75.

Louise was nine years older than Paul. She majored in government at Barnard College in New York, then the sister school of Columbia University, and went on to get a master's degree in social work at the University of Chicago. During World War II she worked for the Red Cross at veterans' hospitals in Atlanta and San Francisco, and later became a social worker at St. Luke's Hospital in Manhattan. She was stricken with breast cancer and died in 1966 at 48 years old.

Ruth and Louise never married. All of the girls were unusually tall. Ruth stood six feet tall, Louise six-one, and Virginia, six-two. In Volcker family lore, height helped explain why Ruth and Louise remained single. "My mother never gave us the message that you had to get married," says Virginia. "You had to get a job and support yourself and I think that was partly because we were so tall."

Virginia, three years older than Paul, studied political science at Wellesley College in Wellesley, Massachusetts, taught fifth grade on a Navaho reservation in New Mexico for a year, and then got a master's in education at the

University of Chicago. At Chicago, Virginia met and married Harold Streitfeld, who was studying for a Ph.D. in clinical psychology. He was very intellectual, she says, and "sort of mysterious in some way." He smoked a pipe, like her father, and, not inconsequentially, he was tall. At six-one, he was within an inch of being as tall as Virginia—unless she wore heels. For a change, here was a man she did not tower over. She could be with him and not feel she stuck out.[12] Virginia taught elementary school in Illinois for several years, then devoted herself to raising their five children. After getting a divorce in 1973, she earned a master's degree in social work at Fordham University and spent 14 years working with troubled children at a Roman Catholic foster care agency in New York. She has been living in Connecticut for years and from time to time gets together with her brother in New York City.

For the Volcker girls, their height was a social curse. In their world, the man was always supposed to be taller than the woman. By the time the girls were 12 or 13, they were already over six feet tall. But at that age, Paul Volcker was no taller than average. And it began to bother the girls. "We were afraid he was going to be the little one of the family," Virginia says. "That would have made it even worse that we had suffered being tall." But, finally, Paul's growth hormones kicked in and at 6 feet, 7 inches, he more than met Volcker height standards.

Being tall was not a blessing for the boy in the family, either. "I was very self-conscious in those days," Volcker says, partly because of his height. It was definitely not a plus. "I think it was a negative, being that tall," he says.

Paul's grandfather, Adolph Volcker, gave the family its

height and its determined reticence. He had come from a big family of big boys, all very tall. He stood 6 feet, 4 inches and weighed 300 pounds[13] and had the bearing of a military commander. He had come to the United States in the late 1800s from the German town of Meppen, near the Dutch border. He worked as a tea and coffee wholesaler and eventually married another German immigrant, Pauline Keyser from Eisennach, near Dresden. She taught school in Hoboken, New Jersey. At first, they lived in Hoboken, where Paul's father was born in 1889; then the family moved to Brooklyn. Paul Sr.'s two brothers were born there and the three of them studied at Boys' High School in Brooklyn. Years later, Paul Sr. spoke proudly of the classical education he received there.

To his grandchildren, Adolph Volcker seemed stiff and autocratic. He sported a handlebar mustache and was once mistaken on the streets of New York as the captain of the infamous German battleship *Bismarck*.[14]

Sometimes, the girls got physical with their brother. As Virginia recalls, it was probably "more pushing him around" than punching him. In any case, she rationalizes, "It was always with the most noble motives," becoming assertive, saying, "if he did something he wasn't supposed to do." The crimes in the Volcker family were never capital offenses. In one of the more serious infractions, Virginia caught Paul Jr. playing with matches. She remembers grabbing them away and giving him a shove. "It was the kind of thing my mother would have done," she says.

Paul remembers his sisters bearing down on him. He laughs about it now, but he says their behavior verged on abusiveness. "I joke about this, but there's some truth in it,"

Volcker says. "They were all so conscious that I was not to be spoiled that they leaned over backwards to abuse me."[15]

Louise may ultimately have ended up having the most influence on Volcker, but their relationship was difficult. "I did not get along with her all that well when I was younger, to say the least," Volcker says.[16] "She was an emotional and, I thought, self-centered person. She wrote extremely well and she was a pretty good artist. She was flamboyant. She had interesting friends—very interesting friends. She was very preoccupied with her own life and I'm sure I annoyed her. And she'd squash me once in a while."

One of Paul's childhood passions was building model airplanes made of balsa wood. There seemed to be hundreds of tiny parts and it took great patience and skill to put them together. When he had the mumps, his mother brought him a new model plane kit every day. One day Louise staged her own Pearl Harbor in the Volcker house and smashed Paul's entire aircraft fleet. "I did something to annoy her," he says. "I got in the way or something. She destroyed all my model airplanes."[17]

Years later, the incident seemed far too trivial for a great economist to be discussing. The memory had simply popped out of Volcker during one of our meetings, and it quickly struck him as silly, lacking in dignity, embarrassing even, certainly not something he wanted to dwell on. He had gotten to the point where he could laugh and joke about Louise's assault on his planes and other childhood bruises. But it seemed that the incidents had not been funny at the time, and had left a lasting impression.

Being the only boy in that household cast Volcker as somewhat of an outsider. "He sort of got lost in the shuffle,"

Virginia says. "We did a lot of sewing. That was one of the things he was not involved in; and shopping and cooking, not the kind of things a mother does with a boy. Except for fishing, my father wasn't interested in sports. So, as the boy, Paul was kind of left out."[18]

Louise especially hogged the family spotlight. "Louise took a lot of attention," Volcker says. "She was always having emotional ups and downs and it annoyed me that she was taking so much attention. I remember I had to listen to all this and calm her down."

Volcker's response was to withdraw into himself. In high school he was in the top of his class and played varsity basketball. But he was quiet and shy. Paul's mother, Alma Volcker, told *Newsweek* magazine that her son's reticence came early. He had to repeat kindergarten, she said, because he was so quiet that the teacher thought he was immature.[19] "His father and I got a report from school complaining that he didn't take part in group discussions," she said. And then, much as her son does today, she added a bit of playful hyperbole, saying, at a time when Paul was 58 years old, that "he hasn't taken part in group discussions in the family since." Paul's best friend in grade school was a very quiet boy in the neighborhood, Harry Johansen. Virginia says they played for hours without exchanging a word.

As Volcker got older, he remained wary of small talk, and it was decades before he mixed easily with women. Dorothea Van Duzer used to walk to high school with Virginia and two other girl friends. Paul Jr. often started for school at about the same time. But, Van Duzer recalls Paul showing no interest in his sister's friends. "Buddy would come behind us and walk right past," she says, "with no acknowledgement of us at all."[20]

As Volcker was heading to college, he began drawing closer to Louise. She would write him letters from her Red Cross job in San Francisco and they would spend time together when they were home for the holidays. "She was very interested in my career and that I made something out of myself," Volcker says.[21] He named his first child Janice Louise after his sister.

Jim Volcker, Paul's son, got to know Louise when she worked as a social worker at St. Luke's Hospital in New York. "She was as extroverted as he is close to the vest and quiet and within himself," Jim says. "She was very creative. She had a very lively hobby in painting. She did landscapes, but kind of abstract landscapes. Growing up, when I was four or five, she would do wood block prints for me of small animals."[22]

—

In Teaneck, the mayor and town council posts were part-time jobs. As the more-than-full-time town manager, Paul's father was the most prominent official. He was the problem solver, the symbol of authority. He ran the town, and the weight of his office fell on the Volcker children. "Your worst fear was that you'd do something that could get you in the newspapers," Virginia recalls. "You had to uphold the family name. We were always very much aware of that responsibility."[23]

As a teenager, Paul Jr. led an especially careful life. Because of his father's position, he assumed he had no leeway.

"Everybody who was anybody knew him," Paul Jr. recalled, "and if I ever did anything wrong, they'd know who I was. When my friends went out knocking out streetlights, I stayed home. I couldn't risk getting picked up. I felt that pressure very strongly."[24]

Paul's father set the standard. Once, after a heavy snowfall, the head of public works in Teaneck sent a plow to clear the Volckers' driveway and the street in front of their house before taking care of the rest of the town. "Paul gave him what for," Dick Rodda remembers. "He said, 'Don't you ever do that again.' He didn't want the appearance that he was getting special treatment."[25]

During World War II, Paul and his father went on a fishing vacation in Maine with some friends from Teaneck. Gasoline was rationed then and the Volckers' friends pooled their allotments to get enough fuel for one car to drive up together. But, concerned that people might suspect that the town manager had somehow gotten an extra ration for the group, Paul's father insisted that he and his son go by train. They had to transfer twice, then hitch a ride for the last 10 miles. They arrived in North Lovell, Maine, at 11:00 P.M.[26]

One winter, Rodda got permission from Paul Sr. to close off 15 hilly streets in Teaneck for sledding. Rodda went to high school principal Charles Steel and told him he wanted to hire 15 of his best seniors as safety monitors.[27] About 10 days into the program, Rodda was summoned to Volcker's office. When Rodda walked in, Volcker got right to the point. "I see you have Buddy's name on the payroll."

"That's true," Rodda said.

"Well," said Volcker, "I want you to fire him."

Rodda did not think the order was reasonable. "I said,

'Wait a minute. You want a good program here and I want a good program. I think we have 15 top-drawer young people to help us provide this and you must have a pretty good reason for asking me to do this.'"

Volcker replied: "Dick, I have three. First, he's my son and therefore he should not be on the municipal payroll. Secondly, I don't know what you're paying him, but whatever it is, there are kids in this town that need it more than he does."[28]

Volcker paused, and Rodda reminded him that he had said he had three reasons, but that he'd given only two. The pause, it turned out, had been for effect. "Dick," Volcker continued, "if you don't fire Buddy I'm going to get someone else to run the rec department."

Rodda went to Paul Jr. with the bad news. "I told him, 'This has to be your last day on this assignment.' And he said, 'Well, is it something I've done?' I said, 'No.' He said, 'Is it something I haven't done?' 'No,' I said, 'it's not that.' Then he said, 'Oh, my father must have said something, right?' I said, 'Bingo. You got it.' And he said, 'Well, that's okay.' And nothing more was ever said."[29]

One thing Paul Volcker Sr. liked to talk about was engineering. Driving on trips around the state, he would turn to Dick Rodda, a frequent companion, and, as they passed a bridge, go into detail about its construction. He liked explaining to his son, too, how things were put together. At these moments, Paul Jr. saw a "very, very patient" man. "He really was intrigued by engineering–civil engineering," Paul Jr. says. "He told me how you build a bridge and all the stresses. He would draw pictures. He always had an explanation for civil engineering projects."

Paul's father also liked to cook. While Mrs. Volcker thought of cooking as a job, for her husband it was relaxation. Paul and the three girls picked up his enthusiasm. "My brother follows recipes," says Virginia.[30] "He loves Julia Child. He likes to try out different things."

At Thanksgiving, Volcker usually cooks dinner for friends. The secret to his succulent turkey, he says, is that instead of cooking the bird on its back, in the conventional way, he flips it over on its breast and, every 15 minutes or so, douses it with a fine port. (Others have come to see the wisdom of this method; now some supermarket turkeys come with a suggestion printed on their wrapper that they be placed in the oven the way Volcker does it.) He also makes a memorable meat loaf and often whips up pasta dishes. Volcker's fettucini Alfredo was a favorite of his wife, Barbara. When they bought their apartment on the Upper East Side of Manhattan, the previous owner left them a Viking professional range, which remains the jewel of his apartment kitchen.

"If you could sit at our Thanksgiving dinner table, those are some of the best memories of the family," says Volcker's son, Jim.[31] "Everybody gathers together. We can sit there quite a while talking about anything. My dad seems to open up quite a bit at those gatherings."

In Teaneck, the Volckers' life centered around their home. They did not belong to the country club and they did not throw big parties. The family usually went to church on Sundays, but they did not go together. Paul Sr., the strong, upright father, went to his church, Christ Church Episcopal; the strong, upright mother and their children walked to St. Paul's Lutheran, just down Longfellow Avenue from their house.

Here was another of those quiet, unstated Volcker family lessons: Exercising personal independence and preference need not cancel out the love, admiration, respect, and loyalty of family and friends. Breaking the mold did not necessarily mean breaking the ties. A family—a person—could be conservative and still be unconventional, following his or her own pursuits. And Paul and his sisters did just that.

Virginia was the first of the Volcker children to be married. But she decided it would be better if it were not a big event. Her parents had not been thrilled by her choice. "My father was always very apprehensive about who we were going out with," Virginia says.[32] "And who might be interested in us and might take advantage of us. He was not exactly protective, but he was very suspicious of our gentleman friends."

Hal Streitfeld, as she puts it, was not a gung ho type of guy. He did not like to go fishing with her dad. He was very much into reading and music, especially classical jazz. He was also Jewish. "That was a little disconcerting to my family," Virginia says. "My parents never quite liked him. They came to accept him more."[33]

Virginia and Harold were married in the Volcker living room. Three clergymen presided: the pastor of Paul Sr.'s Episcopal church, the pastor of the Lutheran church that Virginia, her mother and the others attended, and a rabbi. "I thought the easiest on everybody would be to just have a small wedding," Virginia says.

—

In his years in government, Volcker often found himself working with swashbucklers, masters, or at least lovers of the bold stroke. John B. Connolly, the charismatic former governor of Texas and pal of President Richard Nixon who served briefly as Nixon's secretary of the Treasury and Volcker's boss, is the exemplar. But Volcker believed in caution. He did not lunge into action. His demolition of the Bretton Woods agreement that ended the linkage of the dollar and gold at a fixed rate and his successful attack on inflation were nothing but bold. But both came after careful deliberation. In New York and in Washington, he would spend hours bouncing ideas off a handful of aides. "He would pursue a line of inquiry until he got to the 'I don't know' answer," says Neal Soss, a special assistant to Volcker at the Federal Reserve Board in the early 1980s.[34] "He would not stop questioning you until you said, 'I don't know about that one.' Then he'd say, 'Well, go find out.' This led to some very lengthy evenings of sitting around saying, 'Let's think about this from yet another perspective.'"

As president of the Federal Reserve Bank in New York, Volcker regularly called in four or five of his people on Friday afternoons. "We would just debate the issues," says Ernest Patrikis, then general counsel of the New York bank.[35] "My motto for Volcker is: He never decided an issue before its time."

Neither, apparently, did his father. In a newspaper column about the elder Volcker shortly after his death in 1960, Bob Henderson of the *Teaneck Sunday Sun* said that "Paul seldom if ever made snap judgments."[36]

"If anyone went to him with a suggestion, an idea or a complaint, he'd most likely take a long puff on his pipe, remark that he hadn't thought of it that way, but [that] if the caller would come back on Thursday at 2:00 P.M., he'd have an answer. And he'd have an answer and a cracking good reason for his decision."

The home Volcker grew up in was a home of abundant caution. Perhaps it was his parents' experience of having lived through the Depression, an experience he shared as a child. Or perhaps his parents were simply two people who would have veered toward caution in any case. The children saw it in their father's methodical ways. They heard it from their mother. "What I got from her," Virginia says,[37] "is, 'Okay, today everything is going fine. But you can never be sure about tomorrow. You have to watch out, be cautious.'"

Jim Volcker describes his father as a "very private person." "He doesn't have a large circle of friends," Jim says.[38] "I can remember him telling me when I was growing up as an adolescent that if you can count the number of friends on one hand, true friends, that's a lot. He has about four or five good friends."

The quiet of the father has been difficult for the son to understand and negotiate. "Even at 45, I can say I'm still learning how best to communicate with him," Jim said late in 2003. "He's the kind of person you have to peel like a banana. People might perceive him as aloof. But once you get past the exterior he's a very sensitive person. It takes a while to reach that, depending on the day or his mood."

—

Paul Volcker Sr. may have always been a man of great integrity and thrift. But the job in Teaneck demanded those virtues. The town had gotten into serious financial trouble just as the stock market crashed in 1929 and the country was heading into the Depression. Over nearly a decade, the town's elected leaders had gone on a spending spree that left Teaneck, as the Volckers were arriving, with more than $6 million in debt. In his first three years as town manager, Volcker reduced the debt nearly 30 percent and managed to cut taxes while most other communities in New Jersey were raising them. He produced a master plan for the layout of the town that restricted commercial development and made provisions for creating parks, helping to preserve the small-town character that Teaneck maintains even now.

"His hand, his imprint is so much on Teaneck," says Helene V. Fall, the town manager in 2003.[39] More than half a century after Volcker retired in 1950, the Teaneck town manager still worked in the small, rectangular office just off the main entrance to the Georgian-style municipal building that had been his headquarters. Fall, a short, sturdy woman with a master's degree in public administration from Fairleigh Dickenson University, sat at Volcker's old desk, a slightly scuffed block of maple. A framed charcoal drawing of Volcker, pipe jutting to one side in the style of General Douglas McArthur, looked down at her from one wall.

Frank Hall, an editor of McGraw-Hill trade magazines, served as mayor of Teaneck from 1978 to 1982 and again from 1988 to 1990. He moved to Teaneck in 1949, Volcker's last year as town manager, and he later edited *The Teaneck 100 Year Book,* celebrating the town's centennial in 1995. "I was just a young guy, just out of the service, when I moved to Teaneck," he says. "I saw how the town was run. The guy was fantastic. He was very strict, very tough. He set up a master plan that we're still following to this day."[40]

Volcker saw himself as the conscience of the community, and that led to tensions between him and the elected officials.

"My observation of being on the town council is that after awhile you get to thinking of yourself as the most important person in the world and you want to do favors for people," says Hall. "Volcker was strictly against that."[41]

Eight years into his career in Teaneck and with another election approaching, the stress became too much for Paul Sr. "Things got so mixed up that suddenly I found I couldn't talk," Paul Sr. said.[42] After a brief hospitalization, he was back at work. But, under constant pressure, he suffered several strokes.

Midway through his career in Teaneck, Volcker nearly lost his job. Three of the five council members, including Karl D. Van Wagoner, who had brought him to Teaneck, pressed Volcker to promote one of the town's two police lieutenants to captain. When he refused, saying neither was qualified, the council members made the promotion themselves. But the state's Civil Service Commission vindicated Volcker. The commission reversed the decision, saying the council had overstepped its bounds.

Soon afterward, the same council members ordered Volcker to fire Henry Penney, the town tax collector. This time, when Volcker refused, they suspended his pay and began angling to get rid of him for good. The struggle between the town manager and the councilmen became the central theme of the scheduled elections a month later. All but one of Volcker's antagonists was voted out of office and the election results were seen as endorsement of his management.

Political skirmishes continued in Teaneck long after Volcker was gone. But Helene Fall says the tone Volcker set for town government has survived. "He created an environment where employees can do their jobs without fear of political intervention," she says. "Mr. Volcker set the course for Teaneck as a municipal entity as it is now."[43]

While Paul Sr. was running Teaneck, his wife, Alma, was running the Volcker family. He often had meetings at night and he seldom got going in the mornings before the children were off to school. On Saturdays and Sundays he would drive around town making notes on work that needed to be done in the coming week.[44]

Paul Sr. had met Alma Klippel when he was helping build new locks and bridges on the Erie Canal as an engineer for New York State. Like himself, she was a child of German immigrants. She was an only child; he, the eldest of three sons.[45] Her parents, Elias and Bertha Klippel, had settled in Lyons, New York, and ran a dry goods store. The Erie Canal cuts right through the town.

A few years after Paul Sr. retired in 1950, he and his wife moved to Lyons. He died on Valentine's Day in 1960 at age 70. In 1981, at the age of 89, Alma Klippel Volcker sold their house in Lyons and went to live with her daughter Ruth in Tennessee. Never much involved with possessions, she gradually had pared down her belongings so that when Ruth came to pick her up for the trip south, everything she owned fit into the car. Mrs. Volcker lived with Ruth until her health began to fail. She then moved into a nursing home and died in 1990 at the age of 98.

Many of Alma Klippel's high school classmates went to relatively nearby Syracuse University. But she chose the more elite Vassar College and graduated in 1913 as the valedictorian with an honors degree in chemistry. She stayed on at Vassar as a teaching assistant for a year, then met Paul Sr. and chose family over career.

She studied German at college and wound up more fluent, the family said, than Paul Sr., who had grown up in Brooklyn in a home where German was the first language. Over her years as a wife and mother, she read history, kept up with current affairs, and admired Eleanor Roosevelt. "She was the one who, if you didn't know what a word meant, would have you get up from the dinner table and go look it up in the dictionary," says Virginia Volcker. "I always had the feeling she would have made a great doctor. She was always very good when things happened. She would not get highly emotional, just do what had to be done. She was a very strong person. But she was sort of puritanical, strait-laced in lots of ways. She really made you toe the mark."[46]

The value of public service was a message that infused the Volcker house. "She talked about it all the time," Virginia Volcker says.[47] "It fit in with what my father was doing. You spend your time doing good for people and working for the betterment of the world. They agreed with each other on the importance of service and social values. The idea of being a businessman wasn't sort of what you did. You did good for the world. Business wasn't seen as giving that much of yourself."

Paul says his mother "radiated" the virtues of public service with her pride in her husband and her conviction that by devoting himself to the well-being of the community he was engaged in an ideal way of life. [48]

While Paul's father spent his life in public service, he had one memorable conversation with his son in which he told Paul Jr. he ought to think seriously about a career in business. Paul was never quite sure what prompted the advice, which, in its explicitness, was rare in itself. Maybe, Virginia ventures, it was a moment when their father was under particular pressure as town manager and began thinking that had he chosen a business career, he could have done better financially for his family. But she and Paul knew their father's heart was in public service. He had never shown any real desire to do anything else. For Paul, it was simply an idea that hung out there in hazy ambiguity, and that he totally ignored. A future in public service was inevitable.

CHAPTER SIX

SCHOOL DAYS

In the summer of 1945, the world war that had devastated swaths of Europe and Asia and taken millions of lives was in its last, violent spasms. The Nazis had capitulated in May, and in August the attacks on Hiroshima and Nagasaki with atomic bombs would humble the Japanese commanders.

Paul Volcker graduated from Teaneck High School in May of that year, and in July, with a wartime schedule in effect, entered Princeton University, one of the finest universities in America. He was surprised to have been accepted. Like its rivals, Harvard and Yale, Princeton in the 1940s was open only to young men, the overwhelming majority of them sons of prosperous if not wealthy families, prepared from childhood at expensive private schools like Dalton and Collegiate in New York and tweedy New England boarding schools like Andover, Groton, and Exeter.

Princeton's reputation was intimidating to Volcker. "I

thought places like Harvard, Yale, and Princeton were beyond me," Volcker says.[1] "They didn't take kids like me from Teaneck High School." Had it not been for the war and the great draining away of America's young men, he rationalized, he probably never would have gotten into Princeton, even though he was a top student in high school, a member of the National Honor Society, and the center on the varsity basketball team.

Indeed, as Volcker moved into a room in North Dod Hall, one of Princeton's plainer dormitories, he thought how strangely quiet the Gothic campus seemed. At that point, hundreds of thousands of American men were serving in the armed forces; hundreds of Princeton students were in uniform, scattered around the world in the U.S. Army, Navy, and Marines.

Volcker had only narrowly missed being among them. As he was finishing his senior year at Teaneck High School, he, like many of his classmates, had been summoned by the draft board in Trenton for a physical examination, the precursor to being taken into the armed forces. But at six feet, seven inches, he was judged to be too tall. An army doctor stamped his papers 4-F: unfit for duty. While Volcker may have felt relieved at the time, the rejection later troubled him. He had been sidelined from one of the monumental events of his generation. He was only an inch taller than the acceptable military standard and later he would wonder whether he should have "shrunk down and gotten in."[2]

On August 6, while Volcker was midway through his first semester at Princeton, the United States dropped an atomic bomb on Hiroshima. Three days later, a second bomb destroyed Nagasaki. On September 2, the Japanese formally surrendered in a ceremony on the battleship *Missouri*. Had he been drafted, Volcker muses, he might have been out of the Army in six months or so. It would have been a small price to pay for the distinction that forever eluded him, the badge of service that so many others shared.

Volcker had not been dreaming about studying at Princeton. His father wanted him to go to his alma mater, Rensselaer Polytechnic Institute, a reliable producer of engineers in upstate New York. Paul Jr. applied to Rensselaer and was accepted. But a few weeks before the start of classes there, he wrote to Princeton.

Even the application form that Princeton sent him was intimidating. "It was like parchment paper," Volcker says.[3] He mailed it in, and, a few weeks later, to his astonishment, came a welcoming letter of acceptance. Paul Sr. was not thrilled. He was apprehensive about how his son would fare in the Ivy League, feeling that compared with his own classic Latin education at Brooklyn Boys School, the preparation at Teaneck High School fell somewhat short of what was needed to excel at Princeton. But, as Volcker now remembers it, the decision to go to Princeton was not a major demarcation in the father-son relationship. Neither of them, he says, regarded it as a young man's defiant declaration of independence. Paul just decided to take a shot, it worked out, and he seized the opportunity. But his father could not help but worry. "He kept telling me it was going to be very hard. You know, 'Watch out.' I was going to be with all those smart prep school kids. And I'd find out I wasn't so smart." As he attended classes, Volcker's self-confidence grew. "I found out that wasn't true," he says.[4] "They weren't as smart as my father thought."

Or maybe it was just that Volcker was exceptionally bright. Donald W. Maloney, another Teaneck High School graduate, entered Princeton along with Volcker. Although they had been in the same homeroom at Teaneck High for several years and had been high achievers, they had not been especially close. Nevertheless, they asked to be roommates at Princeton and were assigned a room on the fourth floor of North Dod. Maloney, who went on to medical school and practiced for years as an internist at Abington Memorial Hospital in Abington, Pennsylvania, just outside Philadelphia, was in awe of Paul. So were the other students on their dorm floor.[5] While they hovered over their work, they seldom saw Volcker hitting the books. Yet, his grades were off the charts. Maloney recalls evenings in the dorm with Volcker. "I'd be sitting at my desk underlining in red, then underlining in black," he says. "And there would be Paul lying on his back on his bed, feet propped up on the wall, completely relaxed, just flicking through the pages of his book, just sucking up the knowledge. He never had to study. He just absorbed everything he heard."[6]

Volcker remembers taking notes like other students, but he hardly broke a sweat. "I was very good at regurgitating what the professor said," he says. Although he remembers working hard in his first few semesters at Princeton, Volcker says he "worked less and less hard."

In his senior year, however, Volcker had a close call that could have delayed his graduation, but ultimately changed the course of his life. "This [incident] really startles me to this day," Volcker says. He was studying economics and history at the then newly established Woodrow Wilson School of Public and International Affairs, which blended studies in political science, history, and economics. As a graduation requirement, he needed to write a thesis. But he had been unable to settle on a theme. Finally, with graduation just half a semester away, he hit on the idea of writing about the Federal Reserve. He had taken only one course in money and banking, but the Fed seemed interesting and he cockily thought: Here is something I can knock out in a hurry. He had no sense that he would wind up spending most of his life immersed in the Fed; at the time, his objective was just to graduate on schedule. When he got going, the thesis did not come as easily as he had expected. "I got frantic because I really had to work," he says. "I had to get the damn thing done."

His thesis adviser was Professor Frank D. Graham, a specialist in international trade. Graham was impressed by Volcker and encouraged him. "I would take him handwritten, scribbled chapters and he would comment on them," Volcker says. For most of his time at Princeton, Volcker shied away from the faculty. "I was very bashful about talking to professors," he says. "I didn't think they would have time for me. I didn't take full advantage of the opportunity." But Professor Graham showered Volcker with attention. He urged him to apply for a fellowship, earn a Ph.D. in economics, and become an economics professor. Volcker produced a 250-page manuscript entitled, "The Problems of Federal Reserve Policy Since World War II."

———

In the Volcker household it was assumed that Paul, like two of his sisters, would go on to graduate studies, but he felt no particular calling, no burning ambition, nothing driving him toward anything approaching greatness.

Yet, even without a career goal, he did exceptionally well academically. Now, later in life, he does not especially want to focus on his early thinking about career choices. When I asked him about it, his first line of defense was to brush away a question with a quip:[7]

Q. When you were growing up, what did you want to be?

A. (Laughter.) Fireman. (More laughter.)

Q. Really?

A. Oh, I'm sure I went through that phase. Everybody—every boy wants to become a fireman.

Q. One of your roommates at Princeton, Don Maloney, knew from the time he fixed a damaged bird at age eight that he wanted to be a doctor.

A. I don't remember having had any particular aspiration. I surely didn't have an aspiration to be an economist.

But he does recall one event that might have influenced his career path. When Paul was in high school, his father took him along for some business he had at the state capitol in Trenton. He introduced his son to the governor, and young Paul was impressed. "Maybe at one point," Volcker says, "I thought it'd probably be nice to be governor of New Jersey or something."

Perhaps most of all, the experience underscored the prestige of public service to the young Volcker. Though he spent years navigating Washington, and friends sometimes suggested he capitalize on what became a national reputation, Volcker never took steps to try for elected office. He might have been good at some aspects of electoral politics. The older he got, the more he shed his early shyness and mixed easily with strangers. (In New York, years after he had left the Fed, people would stop him on the sidewalk and thank him for conquering inflation. He actually enjoyed the attention and would chat amiably with them.) He was always a powerful force on the podium, and, of course, his commanding height might have been somewhat of a plus in politics. His many appearances before Congress, and his public relations flair in presenting the antedote to inflation in simplistic terms while proceeding with an age-old remedy, demonstrated the kind of sophistication and guile that elected office seems to demand. But whether he had the skill—or the stomach—to mount a campaign and get elected was an unresolved question.

As he graduated from Princeton, Volcker did know one thing: He wanted more education and he wanted it at a good school. He applied to Harvard and was offered financial assistance at the law school, the graduate school of arts and sciences, and the graduate school of public administration. During most of his life, money would not be a determining factor in his choices. But at graduate school he went with the highest bidder, the school of public administration.

Volcker needed the tuition money, since his father had told him that after Princeton he was on his own. But another reason for his decision—besides being indifferent to whether he studied law or economics—stemmed from his profound shyness. He had a concrete offer of $1,200 a year from the Littauer School of Public Administration, which later became the John F. Kennedy School of Government. The law school and the school of arts and sciences had not committed themselves, but Volcker figured their initial offers would be much lower, and he didn't want to get into potentially awkward negotiations.

The stipend at the Littauer School was fixed. You won the fellowship, you got the $1,200. End of conversation. "If you went to Arts & Sciences or the law achool," Volcker says,[8] "they asked you how much you wanted. I figured they were good for $500 or so. I would not have had the gall to ask them for as much as the school of public administration had on offer. So that determined my decision." Then, unable to resist one of his characteristic dashes of self-deprecating humor, he adds, "That's why I'm not now a lawyer."[9]

The Littauer School was a creation of the departments of economics and political science, a combining of disciplines, much like the Woodrow Wilson School at Princeton. Volcker took a heavy dose of economics at the Littauer School, and ended up with a similar but slightly broader education than if he had gone to the economics department.

Robert Kavesh, an economics professor at the Stern School of Business at New York University, was a classmate in graduate school. He and Volcker were in different programs, Volcker at Littauer and Kavesh in the Graduate School of Arts & Sciences. But they were both studying economics and they became friends.

Kavesh, too, was impressed by Volcker's ability to stay at

the top of the class with seemingly little effort. "There were many students we called greasy grinds," Kavesh says.[10] "They were people you would never see. They were always studying, studying, studying. Then there were others who were so brilliant that they never seemed to crack open a book. Paul was closer to the latter. Some of us would spend vast amounts of time in the Littauer Reading Room. I don't think I saw Paul there twice. If he studied, he may have done it in secret. But I think he just had this natural gift for understanding things."

Volcker had a sense of perspective that set him apart from most other students. "A lot of students were highly technical, econometricians," Kavesh says. "They were very interested in the mathematics of economics. Paul was much more interested in the bigger picture of how things really fitted together. He was always interested in policy rather than the minutiae. We had a lot of people coming in with engineering and mathematical backgrounds. This was not Paul's thing."[11]

After two years at the Littauer School, Volcker received a master's degree and had completed the course work for a Ph.D. in political economy. All that was needed now was to write his Ph.D. thesis. After learning that the Rotary Club was offering scholarships for study abroad, Volcker decided to spend a year in England at the London School of Economics (LSE) and write his thesis there.

The LSE turned out to be a perfect place for Volcker. It put him in the heart of London, a short distance from the Bank of England, the Houses of Parliament, and the Courts of Law; and for the first time he was immersed in a different culture. Volcker arrived in London in the fall of 1951. It was six years after the end of World War II, and the British were struggling. Food was still being rationed and bombed-out buildings still lay in ruins around the city. Just outside the gates of the LSE, the ancient church of St. Clement Danes was a charred wreck, with just the walls and the steeple standing.

The LSE had become a Mecca for up-and-coming young people from Britain's colonies and former colonies in Africa and Asia. Many of the leaders of the newly independent countries had studied at the LSE. George Soros, who made a fortune in currency trading and then spent heavily on philanthropy, and Daniel Patrick Moynihan, the New York scholar and senator, studied at the LSE in the early 1950s, though they did not overlap with Volcker.

Dr. Anne Bohm, a Ph.D. in history, was in charge of graduate students at the LSE in the 1950s and for years later. To her, Volcker was indistinguishable from the few hundred other American students at the university. He lived in a handful of low-rent flats, one of them on Inverness Terrace, not far from her apartment in the Bayswater section of London. But it was not until years later that they became friends.[12]

To Volcker there was more to London than the LSE. As it turned out, he was even less of a grind there than he had been at Princeton and Harvard. He rarely went to classes or seminars and he never got around to writing his thesis.[13] But he developed a deep affection for Britain and traveled around Europe, unconsciously laying the groundwork for a career that would center on international economics.

Sometimes he traveled by train, sometimes by bike. His

entrée was the Rotary Club. "You went from one Rotary Club to another," he says. "They put you up. In England, the Rotary was more like the United States, a middle-class sort of thing. On the Continent the Rotary was a high-class organization. It was a little snobbish in France and Switzerland."

The British social system imposed itself on him. "American students were not nearly as common in England as they are now," he says. "They didn't know what to do with you because in England you were either working class or you were a gentleman." The result was that Volcker and other American students were given a pass to gentleman status.

Volcker did, in fact, do some studying in London and attended the lectures of some notable professors. Dr. Bohm put him under the wing of Richard Sayers, a banking specialist on the faculty who later wrote a history of the Bank of England. Like most of the American graduate students at the LSE then, Volcker was not working toward a degree, but was enrolled as a research student. "Research students at LSE can do what they like," Dr. Bohm said one afternoon in her London apartment.[14] "They can go to any lecture they want. They can read in the library and they write something if they wish—or not. All these big names did that, Pat Moynihan and the others. Very few of them did a Ph.D." Volcker often attended Sayers's weekly banking seminars and sometimes dropped in on seminars given by Lionel Robbins, an economist who later became chairman of *The Financial Times*. "Students would sit around on the floor and reminisce with him," Volcker recalls.

Banking, and money, became central to Volcker. It was in that lone banking course he'd taken at Princeton with

Frederick Lutz, an Austrian who had left his country as the Nazis were gaining strength, where a lifelong interest in banking was ignited. Whatever it was that caught his interest, the seeds were planted by Lutz, as well as by Oskar Morganstern, a Princeton professor who was a pioneer in game theory. At Harvard, Volcker studied money and banking and public finance under Alvin Hansen, a proponent of Keynesian theories of government stimulation of economies and an adviser in the creation of the Social Security system. He studied international trade with Gottfried Haberler, an influential writer on business cycles and on currency exchange rates.[15]

Volcker's thesis was another remarkable element in the journey of a man who even in his later years steadfastly contended that he never had a game plan for his life but merely shuffled along taking things as they came to him, not worrying in the least about succeeding in a career. In retrospect, the theme he chose to write about in London, like the thesis he happened to write at Princeton, could not have been more perfectly arranged as preparation for the job of chairman of the American central bank.

Largely because he spoke only English, Volcker decided to use the Rotary scholarship in London, and since he was going to be in England he decided his thesis would be a comparison of the central banks of Britain and the United States. And, of course, he had already done a fair amount of the heavy lifting in his Princeton paper.

So Volcker decided to look into how the two banks handled interest rates, foreign exchange issues, and regulation. One big difference, he discovered immediately, was that Britain had a half dozen countrywide banks with hundreds of branches, compared with thousands of individual banks in the United States, and that raised a range of questions.

"When you had this highly unitary banking structure in England, how did that affect how loans were controlled, interest rates and regulations and so forth," Volcker says. "I've still got some 5×7 cards where I took a few notes."[16]

The Rotary gave him wonderful access. And sometimes faculty at the LSE would pave the way for him. "I'd call up a bank, say I wanted to see somebody," he says. "I got to see the chairman of the bank, for God's sake." But when Volcker left England at the end of his Rotary scholarship, after 15 months at the LSE, his thesis was still no more than a pile of notes.

Back home in Teaneck, Volcker's parents invited a few of Paul's friends over to celebrate his return. One of them was Donald W. Maloney, his roommate from Princeton. Maloney brought along Barbara Bahnson, the strikingly attractive daughter of a general practice physician in Jersey City, New Jersey. Barbara, a student at Pembroke College, the sister college then to Brown University, met Maloney through her brother, Bill. Bill Bahnson and Don were classmates at the Harvard University Medical School and fellow summer Reserve Officer Training Corps cadets at Fort Sam Houston in San Antonio, Texas.

Barbara had heard a lot about Paul Volcker before she laid eyes on him that night in Teaneck.[17] But nothing had prepared her for the real thing. "Everybody was standing up around the table, and Paul was toasting the Queen," she said.[18]

She was five-foot-seven, exactly a foot shorter than Paul. He was the tallest man she'd ever met. And, to her, this quiet, serious young man with a talent for economic analysis was "certainly the funniest." She felt a spark, and decided

Paul was her man. She got some friends to organize a cocktail party and invited him.[19] "She called me up and said, 'Oh, we just happened to—some friends and I are having a party and we thought you might want to come,'" Volcker recalls.[20] He went to the party. But his interests were elsewhere. "I had a girlfriend at that point," he says. "She was in England."[21]

Distance did not help the London relationship, though, and besides, Barbara was determined. She offered to do some typing for Paul.[22] Finally, he suggested they go out. "It was an uphill fight for two years," Barbara said.[23] In the end, she hit him with a tactic that has done wonders with men over the centuries. "I started going out with someone else," she said.[24] But even then it was Barbara who proposed. "I really went after him," she said.[25] They were married on September 11, 1954.

At the time of his marriage, Volcker was working at the Fed in New York. With seven years of college behind him, he was making $3,000 a year.[26] Barbara, who had gone to work after getting her bachelor's degree, was at Colgate-Palmolive earning only about $500 less[27] as one of the assistants (they were then called executive secretaries) to the chairman of the board of the company, E. H. Little.[28] It was not until years later that economists, even in government service, began to draw much higher pay. Volcker did not have high expectations for the future. Indeed, he told Barbara "that he would never amount to much and would probably wind up working in some dark office as an economist, wearing his green eyeshade and making only $6,000 a year."[29]

The Volckers had no idea what lay ahead for them, but Paul's hunch about his poor earning potential, while exaggerated, was closer to the truth than he could know. The man who would conquer inflation would soon face some of the greatest battles—personal and professional—of his life.

CHAPTER SEVEN

HARDSHIP

Paul Volcker's appointment as chairman of the Federal Reserve Board, one of the most influential jobs in America, was not an entirely joyous event for his family. While settling into his new professional position, Volcker was forced to deal with personal issues as well. His wife and two children, then 24 and 21, recognized the accomplishment, but they all knew that the new job would mean additional hardship for a family that had already endured plenty of adversity. With the new position, the Volckers would be separated for years and strained financially.

Volcker's wife of 25 years, Barbara, had followed him to Washington and back to New York twice, packing up the furniture and china, helping to sell the old house, buy a new one, and build a new social circle. But now, mainly for health reasons, she did not feel she could do it a third time. She had been afflicted with diabetes all her life and by the time Volcker was chosen to run the Fed she was also suffering from rheumatoid arthritis, a painful, crippling disease that attacks the joints and bones. Each of these diseases imposed heavy demands; together, they gradually consumed her life. By the summer of 1979, when President Carter summoned Volcker, Barbara Volcker, at the age of 49, strikingly attractive and as outgoing and entertaining as her husband was reserved, had begun frequently wearing braces on her lower legs and increasingly resorting to a wheelchair.

After their latest move to New York, Barbara met Michael D. Lockshin, a specialist in rheumatoid arthritis, at New York University's Hospital for Special Surgery in Manhattan. Dr. Lockshin, a quiet, engaging man with the wiry build of a cross-country runner and a voice that sometimes dropped to a whisper, treated her arthritis and became her confidant and adviser on virtually everything else. The whole family liked him and he occasionally came to the Volckers' dinner parties, joining such guests as Bill Moyers of public television and Ed Koch, the former congressman and mayor of New York. Barbara could not bear to think of looking for a substitute for Dr. Lockshin in Washington.

There was yet another health concern for the Volckers. Their younger child, James Paul Volcker, had been born with cerebral palsy. He had endured half a dozen surgeries that enabled him to walk haltingly with a pair of canes. But in the summer of 1979, Jimmy, as he was known then, was just coming out of a stretch of depression and anorexia that had begun to take hold in his last year of high school. The illness—a kind of melancholy that was never fully defined, but that Jim later attributed "to the usual adolescent anxieties, combined with my feelings of dealing with the handicap"—led him to drop

Paul Volcker at the Federal Reserve bank in New York as he was named president of the bank on May 1, 1975, with his predecessor, Alfred J. Hayes. (Barton Silverman/*The New York Times*)

Paul Volcker in Cape May, New Jersey, a few months after his birth there on September 5, 1927, in the arms of his mother, Alma Volcker, and one of his sisters, Virginia. (Courtesy Virginia Volcker Streitfeld)

The Volcker home in Teaneck, New Jersey, where Paul Volcker grew up. (Courtesy Virginia Volcker Streitfeld)

Paul Volcker striking a big-league pose in his yard in Teaneck, New Jersey. (Courtesy Janice Volcker Zima)

Paul Volcker, looking out at far right, as a nine-year-old with neighborhood friends in Teaneck and the hut they built from scrap lumber. (Courtesy Winifred Raetz Harris)

Paul Volcker as a graduate student at Harvard University in 1950. (Courtesy Virginia Volcker Streitfeld)

Paul Volcker as a young teenager with his parents and three sisters in Teaneck in 1941. From left: Louise; Virginia; his mother, Alma; his father, Paul Sr.; and Ruth. (Courtesy Virginia Volcker Streitfeld)

Wedding day, September 11, 1954, in Jersey City, New Jersey. From left: Louise Volcker; Paul Volcker Sr.; Ruth Volcker; Paul's mother, Alma Volcker; Paul and his bride, Barbara Bahnson; Virginia Volcker Streitfeld and her husband, Harold Streitfeld. (Courtesy Virginia Volcker Streitfeld)

Paul Volcker with his son, Jim, shortly after birth, and daughter, Janice, at about three years of age. (Courtesy Virginia Volcker Streitfeld)

At Camp David with President Richard M. Nixon at an August 1971 meeting to end the linkage of the dollar to gold. Paul Volcker, second from right, was the principal architect of the change. To his left is Caspar W. Weinberger. The others, seated from far left, are Peter G. Peterson, Arthur F. Burns, John B. Connolly, President Nixon, George P. Shultz, Paul W. McCracken, and Herbert Stein. (Courtesy of The National Archives Nixon Project)

Paul Volcker, as undersecretary of the Treasury, with John B. Connolly, secretary of the Treasury, in November 1971. (White House Photo)

Composite picture published in *The New York Times* on December 31, 1972, along with an article on what the newspaper referred to as "Nixon's all-star economic team." Paul Volcker, then undersecretary of the Treasury, is second from the right in the back row, with Arthur F. Burns to the right and Peter M. Flanigan to the left. The others in the back row, from left, are William D. Eberle, Herbert Stein, Peter G. Peterson, and Roy L. Ash. In the middle row are Frederick B. Dent (left) and George P. Shultz. In front are William E. Simon (left) and William J. Casey. (*The New York Times* archives)

Paul Volcker with his daughter Janice in Paris for a meeting in August 1973 of Volcker, then undersecretary of the Treasury, with Valéry Giscard d'Estaing, then the French minister of finance, later prime minister of France. (AP/Wide World)

Paul Volcker and family at the White House with President Jimmy Carter on August 6, 1979, as Volcker was sworn in as chairman of the Federal Reserve Board. From left: Mary Slowinski, college roommate of Volcker's daughter, Janice; Dr. Conrad Bahnson and his wife, Edna, Barbara Volcker's parents; Barbara Volcker; President Carter; Janice Volcker; Paul Volcker; Jim Volcker; and Christian Zima, Volcker's son-in-law-to-be. Back row: Victoria Streitfeld, Volcker's niece; and Virginia Volcker Streitfeld, one of Volcker's sisters. (White House Photo)

Paul Volcker with Senator Paul Sarbanes, Democrat of Maryland and a member of the Senate Banking Committee, talking before Volcker testifies at a hearing of the committee on October 15, 1979, nine days after he sent interest rates into a steep climb by radically changing the way the Federal Reserve managed the nation's supply of money. (AP/Wide World)

Paul Volcker under fire at a hearing of the House Banking Committee on July 21, 1981, as he declared that even though the country was sliding into a severe recession, he was taking steps that would make conditions worse. He was doing so, he said, for the long-term good of America. (George Tames/*The New York Times*)

Paul Volcker painting the same disturbing picture of further economic hardship on July 22, 1981, at a hearing of the Senate Banking Committee. (George Tames/*The New York Times*)

Paul Volcker with President Ronald Reagan on the steps of the Treasury Department in Washington on January 24, 1981, a few days after Reagan was sworn in as the 40th president of the United States. (AP/Wide World)

Paul Volcker presiding at a meeting of the governors of the Federal Reserve Board in the summer of 1982, at end of table, to the right. (Jim Wilson/*The New York Times*)

British prime minister Margaret Thatcher visiting Paul Volcker at the Federal Reserve in Washington in March 1985. (Courtesy Federal Reserve Board)

Paul Volcker with Alan Greenspan at the White House on June 2, 1987, when President Reagan announced that Volcker was resigning and would be replaced by Greenspan. (AP/Wide World)

Paul Volcker with James D. Wolfensohn on March 2, 1988, after the announcement that Volcker was joining Wolfensohn's small investment banking firm as chairman. (Carrie Boretz/*The New York Times*)

Paul Volcker with Joseph F. Berardino, the chief executive of the Arthur Andersen accounting firm, on February 3, 2002, after the announcement that Volcker would try to revive the firm as accusations were growing that it had helped Enron, the big energy company, conceal huge losses from investors. (James Estrin/*The New York Times*)

Paul Volcker dancing with his daughter, Janice, on her wedding day, September 19, 1981. (Courtesy Janice Volcker Zima)

Paul Volcker with his wife, Barbara, celebrating their 25th wedding anniversary. (Courtesy Janice Volcker Zima)

Paul Volcker fly-fishing in Iceland in the late 1990s. (Courtesy Janice Volcker Zima)

Paul Volcker with two of his grandsons, Michael Zima (front) and Colin Zima in 1989. (Courtesy Janice Volcker Zima)

Paul Volcker with Michael Zima, one of his grandsons, on a fly-fishing outing in Pennsylvania. (Courtesy Virgina Volcker Streitfeld)

out of Brown University after one semester.[1] Thinking he might do better on a smaller campus, he spent a semester at Hamilton College in upstate New York, but it was not to his liking, either. As his father was poised to wrestle the nation's economy, Jimmy was attending New York University in Manhattan and frequently spending the weekends uptown at the Volckers' East Side apartment. He had developed a good relationship with Dr. Peter Kim, his psychotherapist. Given the relative stability that Jimmy now found in New York, it did not seem like an ideal time for him to be moving to Washington, and he was not ready to be on his own. It had been a long haul for Jimmy, particularly during his last year of high school. Finding Dr. Kim had been a blessing.

Back in 1975, instead of going to New York with their parents when Volcker became president of the New York Fed, the children had stayed in Washington. Janice was going into her third year in the nursing program at Georgetown University, and Jimmy was in his last year at St. Albans, the elite Episcopal boys school at the National Cathedral. For the first time, he would be living on the campus as a boarding student. During the first half of Jimmy's senior year, Barbara Volcker remained in Washington, close to the children. Paul lived with Barbara's parents in Jersey City and commuted to the New York Fed in the Wall Street district. When they could, they shopped for a co-op apartment in New York. It was a good time to be house hunting: The city was in the midst of a fiscal crisis and the bottom had dropped out of the real estate market. They wound up with a big apartment in one of the most desirable neighborhoods at a stunningly low price. In early 1976, Barbara and

Paul moved into the apartment on the Upper East Side and Janice and Jimmy were on their own in Washington.

In that last year, something began to go wrong with Jimmy. "I lost a lot of my self-confidence," he said later.[2] He began to think that, because of his cerebral palsy, his friends were preoccupied with the thought that he might stumble and fall—as indeed he often did—and hurt himself. How could they possibly have fun at a party, he asked himself, if they were worrying about his well-being? No one ever raised the issue with him, he said, and he is not sure where he got the idea. But it was real to him.

Jim also started to cut way back on eating. He was 5 feet, 11 inches tall, and, at one point, his weight dropped to 105 pounds, about 40 pounds below normal for him. Had he dropped another five pounds, Dr. Kim was ready to recommend hospitalization.

Jim had tried another psychiatrist before starting with Dr. Kim. Some of Dr. Kim's work, as Jim recalls, was very straightforward. "I was losing weight and my parents were extremely concerned," Jim says. "I was never officially diagnosed, but I had the classic anorexic mind: I was going to get fat and how was I going to work it off? Dr. Kim would say simple things: 'I want you, as you're going around the city, if you're hungry and you see something you want to eat, just go in and buy it and eat it. Don't worry about having to work it off.' Simple things like that. And over time it worked."

Volcker had to fly to Puerto Rico for business in 1978 while he was running the New York Fed, and Jim, still badly underweight, was starting to take a few classes at New York University. He took Jim along. On the way home, they stopped in the Florida Keys to go bonefishing. The trip turned out to be a form of therapy. At every meal, father and son stuffed themselves. "He always made sure we had full meals," Jim says. "They were not necessarily fancy, but we fed ourselves well."

—

Though the family acknowledged the hardship that accepting the chairman's position would bring, they did not spend much time debating the issue. Jimmy was visiting his grandmother in Lyons, New York, on the Erie canal, when his father received President Carter's offer. Volcker telephoned his son with the news. "Of course I was supportive," Jim said later. "I told my father, 'You should do it.'"

Barbara Volcker may have understood the inevitability of her husband's decision even better than Volcker himself. "He is not confident about himself in some ways," she told a reporter for *Time* magazine after Volcker had been chairman for a few years. "But in his field, he is more sure of himself than anybody I have ever known. It may sound egotistical, but I believe that he thinks he is the only man in the country who can do the job. It is the culmination of everything that he has done in his professional life."[3]

At Volcker's swearing-in in the East Room of the White House on August 6, 1979, Barbara, their son and daughter, her parents, and his sister Virginia were at his side. But only Volcker would be moving to Washington. Barbara had decided to remain in New York with Jimmy. "You go," she told Volcker. "I stay."[4]

As Volcker took charge at the Fed, he and Barbara agreed that he would take a shuttle flight home from Washington on weekends as often as he could and that sometimes

Barbara would fly down to spend time with him in the capital. That worked well at the beginning of Volcker's tenure: Barbara would often be in Washington and Paul frequently flew to New York. But as Barbara's health deteriorated and she began to feel less social, the frequency of these visits trailed off. "Over time," their son infers, "I think the stresses that you might imagine would occur with the separation became more evident."[5]

One tension grew out of Barbara's increasing belief that in social situations in Washington, at receptions and dinners, no one really wanted to talk to her. As far as she could tell, she was merely an appendage of the chairman of the Federal Reserve. Volcker and the children tried to reassure her. But she only became more convinced of her own judgment.

"When he was at the Treasury, one thing you remember about her was her humor," Jim Volcker says. "She was chatty in a way that my Dad was not. She could engage anybody in conversation."[6]

Barbara seemed to enjoy Volcker's first two assignments in Washington. "She made friends more easily than I did," Volcker says.[7] "Washington is an easy place to be sociable because there are a lot of new people around and everybody's looking to be friends. And she made a lot of good friends, mostly people who were also in government.

"But when I became chairman and she wasn't feeling so well, she had this syndrome increasingly that many women do, and she had a bad case, that the only reason anybody pays any attention to me is because of you. This is a very common feeling among Washington wives. They don't think they have any identity other than through their husbands. But she had it in spades. She'd come down to Washington once in a while. But she didn't take the pleasure in it that she had earlier. And it was an annoyance to me, frankly, because, first of all, it was nice to have her down there to go to some of these things that I was always getting invited to."

According to her family and friends, Barbara had always had a tart manner. She was not mean-spirited, but she was intolerant of pomposity and immodesty and she did not automatically accept that high office suggested a high-quality intellect or commitment to public service. "She was very good at puncturing pretensions," Volcker says.[8] "But that was kind of nice. She didn't do it in a nasty way. People really liked to be with her at dinner parties, but she just refused to recognize that, even though when she went, she would enjoy herself."

One family relationship actually grew stronger while Volcker was chairman of the Fed. By the time he returned to Washington in 1979, his daughter, Janice, had graduated from Georgetown and was working as an assistant nursing coordinator at the university hospital. She lived across the Potomac River in Arlington, Virginia, and father and daughter managed to see quite a lot of each other. Sometimes when he needed a partner for a dinner at the White House or some other grand occasion and Barbara was not available, Volcker would take Janice.

Despite Volcker's tendency against emotional displays, there were some tender moments between the two. The night before Janice was to be married in September of 1981, she went to visit her father at his apartment in Washington. Her mother was there, too, down from New York. Janice was having second thoughts about the wedding. "I really got the jitters," she says.[9] That night, Volcker and his daughter walked around and around the block, talking and thinking. "We must have walked around the block 20 times," she says. He was the father every young woman would want; he did not push her one way or the other. "He just said, 'Just do whatever you need to do. Go with your heart; it will work out.'" He would be with her, whatever she decided.

The next day, September 19, Janice was married in the National Cathedral to Christian Zima, the handsome brother of her best girlfriend in high school and a sales representative for a company that supplied packaged cuts of beef to hotels and restaurants. She was 26 years old; he was 30 and divorced. They toasted each other at a reception at the exclusive Cosmos Club, where for generations presidents and congressmen and Washington power brokers have gathered. They now live in a rambling home with a big yard in the Virginia suburbs and are the parents of three boys.

—

As Fed chairman, Volcker was recognized by millions of Americans as one of the most powerful figures in Washington, confident and assertive. But the man that Americans saw on television and the covers of national magazines led a strikingly humble private life.

In one of the peculiarities of the Federal Reserve, when Volcker went from being the president of one of the 12 regional banks to being chairman of the entire system, he took a 50 percent pay cut.[10] Oddly, for a man who had risen to a position of influence over every American's money, Volcker had never been particularly concerned about his own pay. He was not a big spender and he always had what he considered to be enough money, at least until his annual salary dropped from $110,000 to $55,000.

Rummaging through some old files in 2003, Volcker came across a pay slip for the first seven months of the year after he'd been chairman for two or three years. It showed earnings of $39,000, suggesting his annual pay had risen to about $67,000. But after federal taxes, District of Columbia taxes, a 7 percent contribution to the federal pension plan, a withdrawal for Social Security, his share of his medical coverage and some other deductions, Volcker's take home pay for about half a year's work came to about $19,000.

On his own in Washington, beyond the marbled corridors of the Fed, Congress, and the White House, Volcker lived more like a graduate student than a prince of power and influence. Some evenings, of course, he was invited for dinner at the White House, and he was a popular extra man at exclusive gatherings at salons around the capital. But at the end of the evening he went home to a bare apartment furnished with an extra long bed, a couple of chairs, a kitchen table, a chest of drawers—just the essentials. He watched the news on a 10-inch black-and-white television set.[11]

In a city where most offices start to empty out around four or five in the afternoon, Volcker was often at his desk into the early evening. On nights when there were no dinner invitations, he would head off to a modest restaurant; one of his favorites was an unassuming place called Marrocco's, where he was likely to order a single domestic beer rather than pay extra for an import.[12] Volcker had been frugal throughout his life, but now, living in an expensive city on a shrunken income with medical expenses at home increasing, he especially had to watch his spending.

One might think, given Volcker's prominence in the world of high finance, that he took his trademark thriftiness a bit too far. His first apartment in Washington was in such a rough neighborhood that he worried about being mugged. After a few weeks, Volcker moved to a one-bedroom apartment on F Street, near the campus of George Washington University. Most of his neighbors in the apartment building were university students, and on some weekends he had to weave around sweating kegs of beer and blaring loudspeakers in the corridors.[13] When Volcker visited his daughter he would take a suitcase stuffed with dirty laundry to run through her washing machine, just as some students did when they went home. The monthly rent in early 1982, after he'd been there for nearly three years, was $394.[14]

But for Volcker, the simple life was no ordeal. "You're the chairman of the Federal Reserve," Volcker says. "You're busy anyway. You could live in a one-room apartment down there. What difference did it make? People would invite you to parties and not expect you to return the hospitality and all the rest."[15] Though almost certainly not something Volcker thought out, the austerity underscored his disdain for materialism and added to his legendary reputation for integrity. But for Barbara there was no reward for coping with a tight budget. "She's sitting up in New York trying to make ends meet and taking care of her son and worrying about him and not having any money," Volcker says. "She felt desperate."

To raise money, Barbara took a job as a bookkeeper and administrator for a small architecture firm in New York. For a while, she rented a room in the Volckers' Manhattan apartment to a man who lived in the suburbs and owned a small printing business in the city.[16] "The strain was on her, not me," Volcker says. "I didn't need any money, because I wasn't spending any money."

It was not an arrangement Volcker would have chosen. But he and the family agreed there was no way he could have walked away from a chance to run the Federal Reserve. He had to do it.

—

Barbara Volcker was seven months old when her father, Dr. Conrad Bahnson, a family physician in Jersey City, New Jersey, realized that she had juvenile-onset diabetes. Now known as Type I diabetes, it is the most severe form of the disease and the least common.[17] In 1930, when Barbara was born, early-onset diabetes was a deadly disease; most people who had it died in their twenties or thirties.

When Barbara and Paul were dating, she would tease—in her edgy way of blending the macabre with the mundane—that they would never get married because she would not be living that long. But the prospects for diabetics had improved markedly. After their wedding, Barbara was determined to have children. It was the 1950s and, like many couples then, the Volckers did not agonize over whether and when to have children. The ethos was that being married meant becoming parents.

But for a diabetic like Barbara, pregnancy and childbirth were extremely risky. Mothers and infants often died in the process, and many children who survived suffered severe side effects.[18] The Volckers knew the risks, but Barbara was encouraged by the success that Dr. Priscilla White had been having at the Joslin Clinic in Boston working with pregnant diabetics. From childhood, Barbara had been treated at the clinic, now the Joslin Center for Diabetes, and at about the time of her marriage she talked with Dr. White about having children.

Within months of her marriage, Barbara was pregnant. The next summer, in late June or early July, in about her eighth month of pregnancy, Barbara checked into the Boston Lying-in Hospital, a teaching unit of the Harvard Medical School that is now known as Brigham and Women's Hospital. Janice Louise Volcker was born on August 20, 1955, in perfect health.

Two years later, encouraged by the smooth delivery of Janice, Barbara was pregnant with James. Again she checked into the Lying-in Hospital well before her due date, but this time things did not go well.

Barbara went into labor early. Further complications developed, and James was delivered by Caesarean section. "It was a big emergency," Volcker says.[19] "He almost died. We didn't know if he was going to live. He was a month or so premature."

Their son, they later learned, was suffering with hyaline membrane disease, a respiratory ailment then common among premature infants. It disrupted the flow of oxygen to the brain. The second son of President John F. Kennedy, Patrick Bouvier Kennedy, had been born with the condition and died within two days in the summer of 1963, a few months before Kennedy was assassinated.

After a short time, James was able to go home with his parents, and at first he seemed to be doing fine. But he did not crawl the way infants usually do, and his parents thought they noticed something unusual about his legs.

"He was eight or nine months old when he was diagnosed," Volcker says. "We took him up to Boston. I don't know whether it was the Joslin Clinic or some other place. But some expert or experts looked at him and told us that he had cerebral palsy."[20]

It was not among the severe cases, and in fact, James' mind was well developed. At age five or six he would occasionally pick up *The New York Times* from the coffee table and read a few sentences. At a nursery school for handicapped children he gave the four-year-old version of a valedictory address on graduation day. But he could not control his legs. He wore braces, and, when he was about five years old, Paul had a wooden rig made of a sheet of thick plywood with two stubby, thick dowels rising from it to enable Jimmy to stand and strengthen his legs. Volcker would take the contraption out to the front yard of their home in Chevy Chase, Maryland, and strap Jimmy in, left leg to left dowel, right leg to right dowel. Then he would hand Jimmy a little baseball bat and begin lobbing balls to him. While hitting the balls was fun for the little boy, it was also a form of physical therapy that added muscle to Jimmy's upper body as well as his legs. "My dad would spend hours with me," Jim says.[21]

When he was four years old, the Volckers sent Jimmy to a nursery school run by the Crippled Children's Society of Washington, D.C. In the mornings there were classes following the teaching philosophy of Maria Montessori; in the afternoons, physical therapy. But the Volckers wanted Jimmy to be in the mainstream. And the sympathetic comments

Barbara endured on Jimmy's behalf—"It's okay, the next one will be fine"—only made her more determined to help him overcome his limitations and lead an independent life.

When Jimmy was six, Barbara spoke to Bob Barrows, the head of the Mater Dei School, a small Roman Catholic boys' school in Bethesda, Maryland. The school had never had a handicapped student, but Barrows decided to give Jimmy a chance. He got along fine and attended first and second grade there while Janice attended public school nearby.

When Volcker left the Treasury and returned to Chase in New York in 1965, the family moved to Montclair, New Jersey, just outside New York City, and Janice and Jimmy went to public schools. Four years later, as Volcker returned to Washington, Jimmy went back to Mater Dei for the sixth, seventh, and eighth grades. For high school, he went to St. Albans. As at Mater Dei, Jimmy was once again the only handicapped student at his school.

"I feel blessed to have been born to pretty enlightened people," Jim says.[22] "They always encouraged me to be as independent as possible, in terms of my mobility and dealing with the able-bodied world. Each of my parents dealt with it in different ways. My mother did certain things for me in a classical motherly way. My dad would be the one, he was sort of tough-love. Too strong at times, maybe. But he was the one who pushed me."

One example of this involves the New York City subway system, a network of tunnels and trains that were new to Jim when he first arrived in New York after graduating from St. Albans to rejoin his parents in their Upper East Side apartment. Jim suggested that he and his dad take a subway ride as a way to become more familiar with the transit system. His father surprised him by replying: "Why don't *you* take a ride?"[23] "That's his style," Jim says. "'You go out and see how you manage yourself' and, the implication was, 'We'll talk about it later.'"

So, balancing on his canes as usual, Jim made his way tentatively down the steep stairs of the subway, bought a token, shuffled through the turnstiles in the strange underground world, and finally boarded a train. "As it happened," he says, "I was fine. And I got to know my way around the subways pretty well. I'm sure my dad loved me just as much as my mother did. He just manifested it differently."[24]

Janice remembered a similar experience with her father when her husband's company scaled back and he lost his job. "He ended up going into business by himself and he hated it and it was sort of one thing after another," Janice says.[25] "I've always felt like my Dad's been supportive. But his response has almost always been, 'Well, okay, pick yourself up by your bootstraps and get going.' You know? 'It's going to be tough. Take a hard swallow and just get going.' It's not candy-coated. He's there to lend an ear, but he doesn't give you a quick fix. He's sympathetic. But he lets you figure it out on your own."

That sympathetic but firm line was very much what America saw in Paul Volcker as he worked to stifle inflation. His measures made life difficult for many people. He knew he was causing pain, but he felt he could not ease up and lend a figurative hand to struggling Americans, as previous chairmen had. To do so, the record suggested, was likely to cause another surge of inflation. So he held steady and, in the end, inflation ebbed and the country was off to one of its longest stretches of prosperity in history.

Volcker's son-in-law could not help but admire the man. But sometimes his sense of propriety was mildly irritating. Shortly after their marriage, with the 1981–1982 recession casting a pall over real estate, Christian Zima and Janice Volcker decided to buy a house. They found an attractive place at what seemed liked a very low price, but they were going to have to pay about 20 percent interest on the mortgage. "He would never help us," Zima says of Volcker.[26] It was not a question of financial assistance. "He would never even answer a question," Zima said, "Like, 'Is this a good time to do this?' He would never answer any of those questions. He would just mumble and change the subject."

When Volcker did extend a bit of advice, it boiled down to: Do the right thing, even if it hurts. At one point, Zima, who is now an addiction counselor, was working for the John Hancock Insurance Company. He got an offer from Cigna, a competitor, and accepted. Then John Hancock countered with more money. Zima remembers Volcker asking him, "Well, did you give this other company your word?"

"I said, 'Yeah.'"

"He says, 'Well, what's your decision then?'"

"I wanted to go back to Hancock because they'd given me a better offer," Zima said later, "but I'd already made a commitment, so I went with Cigna."

Volcker did not suffer high jinks well, and Janice was the rebellious child in the Volcker household. In Washington, the Volckers sent Janice to Sidwell Friends School, a prestigious private high school that has a history of enrolling students from prominent Washington families. At the time, Janice often drove a red Ford Falcon convertible. In a rare extravagance, her father had bought the car for himself. "It was a big deal, I remember, when he bought the car," Janice says.[27] It was not that the Falcon, a very modest car, had been expensive. But, a convertible? A red convertible? He was undersecretary of the Treasury for monetary affairs in the Nixon administration at the time, and it was not the flashy kind of car people in his circle drove. Father and daughter began to share the car. When Volcker used it, he parked in an official lot across the street from the White House with space for the three top officials at the Treasury. At the time, Nixon was in the midst of fighting his way through the Watergate scandal. One day Janice slapped a bumper sticker on the Falcon: "Impeach the President." Volcker, of course, could not drive the car to the White House with that thing on it, and the bumper sticker quickly came off.[28]

Neither Jim nor Janice recalls any specific career advice from their parents. Volcker never suggested they study at Princeton, as he did, or that they consider the field of economics and finance. "I went to him a couple of times and said, 'What do you think I should do?'" Jim recalls.[29] "And he would say, 'It's up to you.' He was always very supportive. But what he would say to me was that you should do what you enjoy. When I was younger that was kind of frustrating."

As a matter of meeting the requirements at New York University, Jim signed up for a freshman course in economics. To his delight, the subject excited him. His father was still president of the Federal Reserve Bank in New York and living in the family's Manhattan apartment when Jim took that first economics course, and he was able to turn to one of the world's top practitioners when he was stumped. "It was great to have my dad home at the time," he says. "He was a great Socratic teacher. You would ask him a question and his answer would be: 'Well, what do you think?' We would spend quite a bit of time talking about economics and specific problems I had and working through them."

In February of 1982, Jim graduated from NYU with a bachelor's degree in economics. He had worked summers at the New York office of the Bank of First Boston and at Schroders Bank & Trust Co. After graduation, he joined Schroders full-time as an economic analyst in the office of Geoffrey Bell, a family friend who was overseeing investments in the United States for foreign central banks. Jim stayed at Schroders when Bell went off to form his own investment firm, Geoffrey Bell & Company, but he eventually shifted to commercial banking at the National Westminster Bank USA.

In the summer of 1992, Jim's life changed in a big way. He was invited to the wedding of a friend, and there met Martha deJong. They were married a year later. Martha still had another year to go at Emory to get her MBA. Jim's solution was to take a leave from NatWest and move to Atlanta. When they returned to New York, his job at the bank had disappeared in the merger of NatWest with the Fleet Bank. He began working as an administrator on a research project at the NYU medical school and eventually received a master's degree from the university in public administration. In 1999, Jim and Martha became parents, adopting an infant girl from China. They also decided to move to Boston to be closer to Martha's family. With the arrival of their daughter, Jennifer, Martha became a full-time mother. Jim, the grant administrator at Children's Hospital in Boston, was the sole breadwinner for his family.

Until he met Martha at the age of 35, Jim Volcker had chosen to live at home with his parents—a frustration for his father. Jim had a good job and money was no problem. Part of the reason was his mother's health. Jim and his mother had grown extremely close during the time Volcker had been living apart from them in Washington. Her health grew steadily worse; she had the first of several heart attacks in the late 1980s while visiting Volcker toward the end of his term as chairman. With his father in Washington and his mother getting progressively worse, Jim felt a strong pull to stay with her. "I felt I couldn't leave," he says. "If I moved out, she would have felt lonely and I would have felt guilty."

His reticence was mainly emotional. Barbara's physical needs were taken care of by others. A woman who had begun as a housekeeper for the Volckers learned to give Barbara insulin injections and watch over her. She was with Barbara every day, and eventually Barbara had nursing care around the clock. When Volcker left the Fed in 1987 and moved back home to New York, Jim was still unwilling to leave. Volcker traveled frequently and Jim took that as justification for staying. "My dad was as present as he could be," Jim says. "But he wasn't there 100 percent of the time."

Jim would see his mother in the mornings, head off to work, and then spend the evenings with her. They talked and kept each other company. "We talked about baseball a lot," Jim says. "She was a great baseball fan. She loved the Mets. They were my team, too, when they were good. Progressively, it was just watching TV at the kitchen table."

Volcker thought his son and wife were developing an unhealthy emotional dependence upon each other. The two of them, Jim and Barbara, realized he had a point. But they could not make a break. "In hindsight, I probably should have been going out doing my own thing," Jim says. "But I felt that if this is social support for my mother, given what she had done for me while I was growing up, I could do this for her. My dad encouraged me to go. I was obviously aware I had to get out. She seemed to like my being there and being a source of support. Yet if you were to ask her, she would also realize she needed to give me my independence. I think she felt very frustrated at her own lack of independence, increasingly, so that she felt conflicted."

Because of Barbara's diabetes, there had been many frightening times for the family. She had developed good instincts about her insulin levels and, like other diabetics, she usually tested blood samples during the day. But sometimes her best efforts failed, and she would go into insulin shock as her blood sugar levels fell. "One thing that happens is you get confused," Volcker said.[30] "You don't quite know what you're doing. You may sweat. You'll get a cold sweat. I guess you get a little weakness after awhile. But mainly you get confused. I mean, this would happen frequently. But when it's severe and there's nobody around, you could lose consciousness. And that happened a few times. You'd get a frantic call."

It happened once when Volcker was at the Treasury and Janice, then a small child, was home with her mother. "She had taken a nap," Janice says,[31] "and when she woke up she began acting crazy. Then she lay back down and I couldn't get her to wake up. I called his office. I didn't know it was an emergency at the time. I can't even remember how old I was. Then I ended up calling back and I said, 'I really think there's something the matter.' They told me he was in a

134

meeting or something. But he got on the phone right away and came home, and then he called an ambulance."

Barbara seemed to have been in a semi-coma. Volcker squirted a sugary substance into her mouth to try to revive her. Sometimes, Volcker would give Barbara a teaspoon of honey or a cube of sugar. "If it was mild," he said, "you'd do it with a piece of candy. If you feel one coming on in time, you take candy. You always have to have candy with you. It would get a little scary. And it's difficult sometimes because she wouldn't be conscious enough to take it and swallow it."

Jim was with her through many of these episodes. "In a severe case she would be perspiring and totally disoriented," he says. "In the middle of the night she would sit and turn on the light and call out: 'Help. I need help.' "

One of the attacks came in the middle of the night when Volcker was in Washington. "I knew what to do from years of experience," Jim says.[32] "But it was still kind of scary for me. I ended up calling my dad at 2:00 A.M. and he kind of coached me through it."

For most of their life together, Volcker and his wife had a close, warm relationship. She was a sounding board and confidante. "He didn't discuss monetary policy and the nitty gritty of the job," Jim says.[33] "But in terms of career moves and impact on the family, he would talk about things like that. In terms of dealing with different personalities on the Fed board, that kind of stuff, she was very good at listening. And she was smart enough to offer good advice. She was very supportive of his work. He had a tendency to pace and talk at the same time and I remember my mother sitting there and listening to him and discussing things. To that degree, it was a real partnership."

135

One common result of Type I diabetes is arteriosclerosis, a narrowing and hardening of the arteries. Sometime in the early 1990s it began to affect Barbara's mind. "She wasn't getting enough blood to her brain," says her brother Bill Bahnson, a retired psychiatrist.[34] Because of the rheumatoid arthritis, she was also often in a great deal of pain. Gradually, the spunky, determined woman that Volcker and the children deeply loved became a different person, transformed by degenerative forces that no one could stop. She became harsh. "She could be mean, biting people's heads off," Jim says. "She could really lash out," says Janice.

It was puzzling and hard for everyone, including her daughter, the trained nurse. "I never quite understood," Janice says,[35] "if my mother's anger was—in the end—organic, or if it was depression, or if it was anger at something that she just couldn't control anymore. I don't know what it was. Of course, it was really hard to take when you were right in the midst of it. But you could step back and say, 'Okay, I understand where this is coming from,' but my dad had to live with it day in and day out. And I don't know how he did that."

Volcker did what he always did. He stayed the course. "People get sick," he says.[36] "The person gets angry and upset, isn't communicating maybe and doesn't want to communicate. It's a mess."

The distress, the changed personality, went on for five years or so. Barbara died on June 14, 1998 at 68 years old. She had been on the brink for months, but her death nonetheless hit Volcker hard. Janice had seen her usually controlled father emotionally shaken only one other time, when his sister Louise died.

Shortly before Barbara's death, Volcker, who by then had earned a healthy salary in his post–Federal Reserve career as an investment banker, decided to create a unit at New York's Hospital for Special Surgery in her memory. With a $1.5 million contribution,[37] he established the Barbara Volcker Center for Women and Rheumatic Disease; Dr. Lockshin, her favorite doctor, agreed to become the director. It has become a base for his research on rheumatoid arthritis and other autoimmune diseases and on why they befall women much more frequently than men.

CHAPTER EIGHT

DIFFICULT CHOICES

On a mission to conquer inflation, Volcker started off as chairman of the Fed with a bang. To a large extent the battle was psychological: If Americans thought inflation was going to continue to be a way of life, as it had been since the days of the Vietnam War, they would keep driving up prices and demanding higher wages to stay ahead of the game. Some Americans were making money off inflation.[1] But Volcker knew that runaway inflation was ultimately destructive, because at some point money became worthless and the economy collapsed. No one knew exactly where the breaking point was, but with inflation already running at an annual rate of about 13 percent, Volcker was deeply concerned.

As he saw it, he was the sheriff called in to restore economic order. His job was to convince Americans that inflation was being crushed and that they no longer needed to keep spending for their own protection. He thought of it as changing people's expectations. If they began to think that prices would not keep going up, they would no longer be rushing to stay ahead of the spending curve.

The danger—and, some of Volcker's critics said, the probability—was that people simply would not cut back on spending until they were forced to; in other words, not until the economy stalled, a lot more people lost jobs, and those people just could not maintain their old patterns. "You hope to get such a change in expectations that you have a minimal effect on actual economic activity," Volcker says.[2] But one way or another, he was going to try to break the fever. In his scenario, prices and interest rates would then begin to fall, there probably would be at least a mild recession, and then, hopefully, an orderly recovery.

Eight days after taking the oath of office, Volcker struck his first blow, leading his colleagues on the Federal Open Market Committee in a vote on August 14 to sharply raise the key federal funds rate—the interest rate that banks charge each other for loans. No one outside the Fed could be sure how much rates had been raised because in those days there was no official announcement for several weeks on decisions by the Committee for fear that abrupt news could shock the markets.

But all the big banks had Fed watchers whose job was to monitor the trading in government securities and determine which way the Fed was pushing the economy and by how much. On August 15, as the Fed began selling Treasury bills and thus reducing the amount of money in the banking system, Fed watchers reported that the Fed appeared to have raised its federal funds rate by one-quarter of a percentage point, to 11 percent. Although they were off by a quarter of one percentage point on the low side, they clearly received the signal Volcker was sending.

Chase Manhattan Bank in New York and Continental Illinois National Bank in Chicago immediately matched the increase in magnitude. Up until then, they had been lending money to their best corporate customers at 11¾ percent, as usual somewhat higher than the federal funds rate. Now they shifted what was known as their prime rate to 12 percent. Soon banks around the country were applying this new rate.

On August 16, Volcker convened a meeting of the seven-member Federal Reserve Board that resulted in an increase in another category of interest rates: the discount rate, the amount of interest the Fed itself charges for loans to banks. It was a rise of half a percentage point to 10½ percent. Not surprisingly, the commercial banks' prime rate stayed at 12 percent. The Fed's discount rate was considered less significant than the federal funds rate. But it was routinely announced within hours of a vote, and it provided Volcker with a tool for publicly underscoring his determination.

John D. Paulus, an economist at Goldman, Sachs & Company and a former staff member at the Federal Reserve Bank of Minneapolis, explained the move for *The New York Times* on August 17, 1979. It was "a signal to the markets that the Fed does not intend to reverse its stance," he said.[3] After years of the Fed backing off just as interest rates reached a threatening level, Volcker realized that he had to drive home the message that, this time, the Fed would not relent. The two rate increases by Volcker's Fed were enough to send the prime rate climbing to a new record level of 13 percent over the next month, a full percentage point above the previous high of 12 percent reached during the recession of 1974–1975.

The higher prime rate was just what Volcker wanted, but a few days later, on September 18, he hit a wall. Volcker urged the Federal Reserve Board to raise the discount rate another half percentage point to 11 percent. The board complied, but this time the vote was split four to three. The mixed signal that resulted was not what Volcker had in mind. But he did not realize he had a problem until the newspapers spelled it out for him: Perhaps further rate increases would be impossible. The feeling among the dissenting board members was strong, and it would take the opposing vote of only one more board member to derail Volcker's plans.

The three dissenting board members made it clear that they worried that the latest rate increase was a step too far, that it could deepen a recession without necessarily halting inflation. "There is some point at which interest rates contribute to inflation rather than restrain it," Nancy H. Teeters, a Carter appointee and one of the members voting against the rate increase, said at the time.[4]

Whether or not a recession was under way was unclear. Economists at the Fed and elsewhere had been describing troubling signs for months, yet Volcker had his doubts. A recession, of course, is political poison. No president wants one, especially Jimmy Carter, who was gearing up for a reelection campaign in the coming year. Volcker may have been predisposed to minimize evidence of a recession, not wanting to accept signs himself that he was being too aggressive.

In testimony before the House Budget Committee in September 1979, Volcker said there was much more danger in "prematurely anticipating the most unfavorable hypothesis"— a deep recession—"than in dealing in the most orderly and effective way we can with the clear and present fact of inflation."[5]

The value of the dollar in relation to other currencies was another element in America's long affair with inflation that confounded Volcker and others before him. The problem involved investment from abroad and international trade, each of which could contribute to worsening inflation.

Rising prices undermined the value of United States government securities and reduced investments by foreigners. United States government securities were considered among the world's safest investments, but a German corporation would not want to invest in Treasury notes paying 11 percent if, say, inflation was running at 13 percent. The corporation would be losing 2 percent on the deal. This weakened the dollar. The reason was that in order to buy United States securities, investors in other countries had to buy dollars with their own currencies. If inflation in the United States were reducing the return on government securities, the investors would look elsewhere to put their money. They would not be buying dollars, and therefore, with less demand, the value of the dollar would fall.

The value of the dollar was important to American policymakers for two reasons beyond mere civic pride. If it were low in comparison to other currencies, United States products would seem cheap to international customers. This would be good for American manufacturers and for the United States' balance of payments, but it would drive the leaders of other countries crazy because it could hurt their manufacturers. American policymakers had to be concerned about the problems a weak dollar created for other countries because Germany, Japan, and other giants could retaliate by imposing barriers to American imports. In fact, what the other countries did most often was not retaliate with sanctions but buy dollars and stow them away in their central banks. This increased demand for the dollar and bolstered its value, keeping the prices of American goods more or less on a par with, or even higher than, products made in other countries. But this intervention, as the bankers called it, could eat up a lot of foreign currency and lead to complaints that the United States should find a way to keep the value of its currency more in line with that of other countries.

Moreover, a dollar weakened by inflation could lead to more inflation. Unless foreign manufacturers accepted less profit, prices in the United States for cars made in Japan and Germany and wine from France would probably rise as a weak dollar bought fewer yen or marks or francs, and with the prices of imported goods increasing, American businesses might safely raise their own prices. Volcker knew that a weak dollar complicated the fight against inflation and ultimately made matters worse for Americans at home. His solution for both inflation and the weak dollar was the same: Raise interest rates.

Yet most Americans in their daily lives had nothing to do with foreign currencies, and whether or not the dollar was relatively strong or weak seemed remote to them. They did not necessarily see inflation and the strength of the dollar as intertwined. Instead, their tendency was to regard the raising of interest rates as harmful to them and as a kind of gift to other countries by making foreign products more competitive in the huge American market and making American-made goods more costly overseas.

After the split decision at the Fed on September 18 over raising the discount rate, Rep. Henry S. Reuss, a Democrat from Wisconsin and chairman of the House Banking Committee, spoke up for the people. From where he sat, the resistance to higher interest rates looked good. "For the first time," Reuss said, "Fed members are wondering out loud whether it really makes sense to throw men and women out of work, and businesses into bankruptcy, in order to 'rescue the dollar' by chasing ever-rising European interest rates."[6]

When the board split over the discount rate, Volcker believed that the three board members who had voted with him were strongly in his camp and that a defection was extremely unlikely. "I knew we had the four votes and if I wanted to increase the discount rate again I would still have four votes," Volcker says. "It didn't particularly bother me." But his confidence was not enough. "The market read it differently," he says.[7] He was going to have to demonstrate to Wall Street and the rest of the country that the Fed was sticking to its guns. "I decided right after that, that we ought to think about some ways to shake this up a bit," Volcker says.

—

In the middle of his second month as Fed chairman, Volcker began developing a strategy for implementing what would be the single most important decision of his career. His insight, triggered by the reaction to the close vote, was that as confident as he felt at the moment, there might very well be a point, before inflation had been stopped, at which a majority at the Fed would say, No more. "When you have to make an explicit decision about interest rates all the time," Volcker said years later, "people don't like to do it. You're always kind of playing catch-up. I wanted to discipline ourselves."[8]

His solution, which now seems breathtakingly simple, was to take the cutting-edge decision out of the hands of the members of the Fed—or at least make it seem that way. Under Volcker's new plan, the Federal Open Market Committee would end the practice of setting the most influential interest rate. Instead, the members would establish targets for the supply of money in the American economy and permit the supply of money to determine the federal funds rate. The board would retain the discount rate as a largely symbolic tool, but the emphasis would be on the money supply.

Historically, after the Federal Open Market Committee determined the interest rate, the Fed's trading desk in New York went to work buying or selling government securities to raise or lower the supply of money to the level required to reach the desired interest rate. Volcker's plan turned the procedure on its head: Instead of the rate determining the supply of money in the banking system, the supply would determine the rate. It was still a matter of supply and demand, and the end result would be the same: An increase in supply would tend to lower rates; a drop in supply would raise them.

The real genius of Volcker's approach was that the interest rate would seem to take on a life of its own and merely settle at a point dictated by the supply of money. The effect was to distance the Federal Reserve from the dread act of directly raising interest rates and to underscore for Americans that inflation was very much about supply and demand. "They'd all been imbued with the idea, which obviously had some validity, that too much money creates inflation," Volcker says, "and the way to control inflation is to control the money supply."[9]

Economists had been talking about dealing directly with the money supply in this way for years. Volcker himself had touched on it in rather technical terms in a speech or two and there had been some enthusiasm for the approach in Congress. But no one had ever actually tried to implement what Volcker envisioned.

An entire school of economists, led by Milton Friedman, the Nobel Prize winner from the University of Chicago, advocated influencing the economy directly through the money supply. But Volcker was not considering the Friedman approach. Friedman argued that the money supply should be increased at a steady rate that roughly kept pace with the overall growth of the economy. Volcker was not going to do that—he was in crisis mode. His targets could not be steady. They had to shrink as a counterpoint to rising demand. As the money supply tightened, interest rates would rise, the economy would slow, and maybe inflation would halt.

One of Volcker's first steps was to speak with Stephen H. Axilrod, his staff director for monetary and financial policy. Axilrod worked closely with the Fed's trading desk in New York to see that the policies adopted in Washington were being carried out as expected. He also monitored the dollar in world markets. Volcker and Axilrod usually spoke two or three times a day. But this was something special. "I've got this idea," Volcker told Axilrod. "You flesh it out a little bit and see how it goes."[10] Together with Peter D. Sternlight, who ran the Fed's trading operation in New York, Axilrod drafted a paper detailing Volcker's plan. "I wrote the general stuff and Peter Sternlight wrote the structure," Axilrod says.[11]

Volcker quietly began building support for his plan within the Federal Reserve. He wanted a public show of solidarity from the six other members of the board and the five presidents of regional banks who, along with him, collectively made up the Federal Open Market Committee. "To make this kind of change you would obviously want full and enthusiastic support," Volcker says.[12]

At first, Volker moved cautiously, worried that "leaks, uncertainty, opposition in the government, all kinds of things" could preempt him. But once the pieces were in place, he planned to strike swiftly.[13]

Emmett J. Rice, one of the members of the Fed then, remembers speaking with Volcker. "He'd didn't go around saying, 'Well, I have a plan to present to you guys and I'd like to know if you agree or disagree,'" Rice says.[14] "I'm sure he did it with everybody the same way he did it with me. We sat down and discussed monetary policies and the difficulties facing us at the time and which techniques and controls were likely to get the best results. He knew very well where I stood. He didn't ask me, did I agree with him? Should we do this? He knew I was with him on this."

On Saturday, September 29, 1979, Volcker, G. William Miller, the secretary of the Treasury, and Charles Schultze, the chairman of President Carter's Council of Economic Advisers, flew to Europe for the annual meeting of the International Monetary Fund and World Bank. On the way in an Air Force plane, Volcker sketched out for Miller and Schultze what he had in mind. "They were not enthused," Volcker said.[15]

Both Miller and Schultze worried about the impact the

plan might have on President Carter as he campaigned for reelection in the following year. Miller was concerned that setting targets for the money supply instead of specifying interest rates would lead to wide swings in the rates and perhaps feed further inflation. For Schultze, Volcker's plan looked like a guarantee for a recession.

From the plane, Volcker phoned Washington to see how Axilrod was coming with his draft of the plan. "There was so much static I couldn't understand a word he was saying," Axilrod recalls. "All I would say is, 'Yes, Paul, sure. Yeah! Sure.' I didn't know what I was saying 'yes' or 'sure' to. Paul's kind of a restless man. And I'm sure he was up there worrying, 'Now, is this guy Axilrod doing the right thing or not?' So he called and I reassured him."[16]

On the way to the banking conference, held that year in Belgrade, Yugoslavia, Volcker and the others stopped in Hamburg, Germany. They spent four hours with Helmut Schmidt, the chancellor of West Germany, who, as Germany's Finance Minister, had worked closely with Volcker in the early 1970s when Volcker was undersecretary of the Treasury for monetary affairs. Another old friend of Volcker's, Otmar Emminger, then head of the West German central bank, and Hans Matthofer, the German economics minister, joined in the discussion at Schmidt's home.

Schmidt was disturbed that the weak dollar was upsetting international trade in favor of American business. In the previous 10 days, the dollar had declined 4 percent against the West German mark.[17] The dollar had weakened against other currencies as well. "Schmidt was at his irascible worst—or best, depending upon one's point of view," Volcker said.[18] "He dominated the conversation and left no doubt that his patience with what he saw as American neglect and irresolution about the dollar had run out."

Schmidt's history of friendship and support for the United States sharpened his argument for the Americans. This was not just any world leader spouting off. In Belgrade, the Americans heard more of the same from central bankers of other countries: Something had to be done about the dollar's weakness. It added further urgency for the solution that Volcker was preparing. Higher interest rates could reduce inflation and strengthen the dollar.

At the conference, Volcker spoke privately with two old friends from other central banks. Off to one side at a reception given by the Deutsche Bank, he chatted quietly with Emminger, the president of the German central bank, and Karl Otto Poehl, who had been designated as Emminger's successor.[19] Volcker hinted at what he had in mind and they seemed supportive.[20]

Volcker left the Belgrade conference early, on Tuesday, October 2, touching off speculation that he was rushing back to Washington to devise a response to the criticism over the weakness of the dollar. When the dollar had plunged a year earlier, Volcker, as president of the New York Fed, had been one of the principal players in putting together a package of $30 billion in foreign currencies to strengthen it.[21] The bankers at the Belgrade conference and the journalists reporting their sentiments thought Volcker was up to something similar. Volcker has always insisted that he went home to finish the plan he had put in motion before heading for Europe. "I was a little itchy because I wanted to get this thing on the road," he says.[22]

Though Volcker has consistently said his priority was domestic inflation, raising rates to squelch inflation also would directly answer the prayers of the foreign leaders and private bankers who were screaming about the weak dollar. It was no wonder they thought the main reason for Volcker's early return to Washington was the trade issue, because that was their main concern. They were proven wrong about Volcker's primary motive, but they got what they wanted—not through an intervention in foreign exchange as they expected, but through an entirely different and surprising method.

Back in Washington, Volcker went over his plan again with Axilrod. Volcker decided that as significant as the shift in tactics on the money supply and rates was, he needed more bells and whistles. After all, he was working on expectations, what was going on in people's heads about this inflation business. "I thought that in itself, as an innovation, it would not necessarily carry the message we wanted to carry," he says.[23] "It might be the most important thing we were doing, but you know, what would the press make of, 'Fed Talking Money Supply'? Well, we'd been talking the money supply in one sense all along, not very successfully. 'Fed Changes Operating Technique.' That's page 13 of the business section. I wanted to move the story at least to the front page."

So he devised a three-point package. Each element could genuinely be seen as a significant step toward fighting inflation, but, taken together, they unquestionably made the booming statement Volcker was after. Provided he got the support he needed, Volcker planned to lead off with something familiar, but dramatic: a 1 percent jump in the discount rate, the largely symbolic rate that the Fed charges banks for loans. Rate increases in both the discount rate and the more influential federal funds rate had historically been administered at an eighth, a quarter, or sometimes a half a percentage point at a time. Only once had the Fed increased rates a full percentage point: the previous fall, when it was trying to reverse a sharply falling dollar. The jump was intended as a jolt then and it was intended, again, to underscore a determination to force economic change. For the next piece, Volcker would require the banks to increase their reserves. This would reduce the amount of money they would have available to lend and help tighten the overall money supply. It would also reduce bank profits. Finally, Volcker would get to the part about focusing on the money supply and permitting interest rates to find their own level.

The new approach was never intended to be entirely freewheeling in the sense that there would be no ceiling at all on interest rates, or that, as Peter D. Sternlight, the manager of the Fed's securities trading operation in New York in 1979, puts it, there would be an "absolutely unguided course for rates." If Volcker's plan were endorsed by the others at the Fed, Sternlight would be in charge of implementing it. "He wanted to have a device that let rates go considerably higher," Sternlight said of Volcker. "I think he felt they had to go considerably higher and I think it made it a more salable approach to say, 'Well, we're just letting the market set the rates.'"[24]

Volcker decided he would orchestrate a vote on his plan on Saturday, October 6, believing he had the support of the six other governors of the Federal Reserve Board and that the five voting presidents of the regional banks on the FOMC would be on board. "We wanted to have it on a Saturday because all the markets were closed and that was the obvious day to have the vote," Volcker says.[25] "We'd minimize the uncertainty in the market; give the market a chance to understand it and so forth." Volcker also knew that the reaction of the markets aside, the Fed had rarely, if ever, taken action on a weekend and that the timing of the event would heighten the drama of what he expected would be the announcement of a blockbuster anti-inflation package.

When Miller, the secretary of the Treasury, and Schultze, the chairman of President Carter's Council of Economic Advisers, returned from Belgrade on Thursday, they were still cool to Volcker's plan. Volcker's thinking was way outside the norm, far too bold and dangerous, fraught with the potential for any number of unpleasant surprises. No one on President Carter's team wanted more uncertainty as they prepared for an already uphill reelection battle.

Miller and Schultze tried to block Volcker. In an interview with William Greider, Schultze said it was obvious something had to be done about inflation and the weakness of the dollar. "My objection," Schultze said, "was that once you do this, you can't back out. Once you tell the world this is the money target and we are going to follow it no matter what happens to interest rates, you have to stick with it and you have no flexibility."[26]

Yet, that was precisely why Volcker wanted the change. He wanted to remove the flexibility, suspecting that persuading his colleagues at the Fed to keep pulling the trigger on higher rates would prove impossible as the thunder of public protest inevitably rose. Before battle fatigue hit the troops at the Fed, Volcker wanted their fingers off the trigger.

Schultze concluded in his conversation with Greider that Volcker was making a political, rather than an economic, move. "In theory," Schultze said, "the Fed could have kept on raising the bejesus out of the interest rates, but that's what it couldn't do politically. The beautiful thing about this new policy was that as interest rates kept going up, the Fed could say, 'Hey, ain't nobody here but us chickens. We're not raising interest rates, we're only targeting the money supply.' This way they could raise the rates and nobody could blame them."[27]

Volcker could not deny that his plan put some distance between the Fed and interest rates, but in an uncommon flash of anger he contended that he never tried to trick anyone. "There's a very cynical view that this is just a way to avoid, to fool the public," Volcker says. "I entirely reject that."[28] But, he adds, "It is true that I thought this was a way of getting ahead of the ball instead of behind the ball. People don't like to raise rates. They'd much rather lower interest rates."

Rather than change the way of fighting inflation, Miller and Schultze suggested the Fed announce a spectacular 2 percent increase in rates. They told Volcker that President Carter agreed with them. Volcker said he would be happy to speak with the president directly, but the two aides said that would not be necessary. Volcker thought it was significant that Carter, who was being kept abreast of the discussions, did not call him over to the White House. "My reading of the situation," Volcker said, "was that while the president would strongly prefer that we not move in the way we proposed, with all its uncertainties, he was not going to insist on that judgment in an unfamiliar field over the opinion of his newly appointed Federal Reserve chairman."[29]

Volcker consulted Anthony M. Solomon, the undersecretary of the Treasury for Monetary Affairs. They had worked together off and on since the 1960s when Volcker was first at Treasury. Six months later Solomon, with Volcker's endorsement, would take Volcker's old job as president of the New York Fed and be at Volcker's side in Federal Open Market Committee meetings in Washington as vice chairman of the committee. At Treasury, Solomon's main concern was the stability of the dollar. He had been the point man on what some referred to as the "dollar rescue" operation, a year earlier. He, as much as anyone, knew that the United States had to respond to the clamor from abroad and strengthen the dollar. While Volcker stressed the fight against inflation at home, Solomon knew that the Volcker plan would also buck up the dollar. Volcker said Solomon "advised me to go ahead if I really felt strongly."[30]

Volcker marched ahead. Worried about a leak and guarded by nature, he held his cards close to his vest. Now, with Saturday quickly approaching, he notified the six other Fed governors and the 12 regional presidents around the country of the meeting, even though only 5 of the presidents, as usual, would be voting. Some of them had to hustle to get to Washington. One board member, Emmett Rice, had gone to New Orleans to make a speech. "I was informed late Friday night that there was going to be a meeting the next day and that it would be good if I could get back," Rice says. "I got back, but only after the meeting had started."[31]

157

The meeting was held in the long, rectangular Federal Reserve boardroom. Volcker stepped through a door connecting directly to his office and took his place at the head of the 34-foot-long polished wood conference table, the marble fireplace to his back. Except for Rice, who joined the group later, the governors and the 12 regional presidents took their usual seats around the table. Early morning light streamed through the windows to Volcker's right. At the foot of the table, Fed economists and other staff members filled several rows of straight-backed chairs. High on the wall behind them, stretched across nearly the entire width of the room, was an immense map of the United States showing the Federal Reserve districts. Stephen Axilrod, who also served as the staff director of the Federal Open Market Committee, sat at a little side table at the other end of the room, near Volcker.

At least some of those who would be voting that day did not know why they were in the room. Larry Roos, the president of the Federal Reserve bank of St. Louis—a center of support for targeting the money supply rather than setting interest rates—told William Greider he had neither been briefed nor lobbied before the meeting. "We were summoned to Washington and none of us knew a damned thing," he said.[32]

Volcker began speaking. Slowly and with the same kind of absence of pressure that works so well for the most successful salespeople, he brought the room to consensus. The issue before them was grave. It required careful deliberation. "I spent a good part of the meeting insisting that before we voted, the consequences must be fully understood," Volcker said.[33]

Frederick H. Schultz, a former state legislator from Florida and a member of a wealthy banking family, was the vice chairman of the board. "Paul was masterful" in the meeting, he told Greider.[34] "I knew exactly what he was doing. The others ended up arguing with him, talking him into doing it. By the end of the day, he had them fully committed." Two votes were required, one by Volcker and the six other governors, the other by the full Open Market Committee that comprised Volcker, the governors, and the five regional bank presidents. Both votes were unanimous.

The meeting ended at about 4:00 P.M. Joseph R. Coyne, Volcker's spokesman, suggested that he and two aides start telephoning reporters for a 6:00 P.M. press conference.[35] By the time Volcker was ready to speak, at least 50 reporters had assembled. *The New York Times, The Washington Post,* the Associated Press, and all the television networks were represented. Coyne had spoken with an assignment editor at CBS who had a problem: Pope John Paul II was in Washington that day. The CBS editor had scheduled his only camera crew to be with the Pope at 6:00 P.M. What was he going to do?, the editor wondered aloud to Coyne. "Send your crew here," Coyne recalls telling the editor. "Long after the Pope is gone, you'll remember this one."

The next day, Sunday, the Fed's changes were front page news around the world. Having failed to talk Volcker out of his new approach, the Carter White House declared its strong support. The Volcker initiatives would "help reduce inflationary expectations, contribute to a stronger United States dollar abroad and curb unhealthy speculations in commodity markets," said Jody Powell, President Carter's press secretary, in a statement shortly after the press conference at the Federal Reserve.[36] "The Administration," he continued, "believes that success in reducing inflationary pressures will lead in due course both to lower rates of price increases and to lower interest rates."

During the week before the Fed decision, the price of gold shot up to a record high of $444 per ounce[37] as the value of the dollar slipped lower. While Volcker insisted that domestic inflation was his overwhelming concern, the pressure on the dollar helped him get majority support for his plan in the long meeting on Saturday.

Emmett Rice had been one of those voting against raising the discount rate in mid-September. He had indicated before the meeting on Saturday that he favored Volcker's new tactics, but he told Steven Rattner of *The New York Times* that the latest international developments had influenced his final vote. "There's been a good deal of instability in the financial markets, in the foreign currency markets and in the gold markets," Rice said.[38] "These conditions have been much more unsettled than I expected."

There had also just been a report of a decline in unemployment and another rise in inflation that bolstered support for Volcker. The improvement in jobs suggested that money could perhaps be tightened without dire consequences—yes, there might be a recession, but maybe it wouldn't be that grim—and the worsening of inflation raised the volume of the tolling bell that everyone at the Fed had been hearing.

A surprise for international bankers and currency and commodities traders was that Volcker took no new steps to strengthen the dollar by intervening in the markets, selling foreign currency and buying dollars.[39] Instead, he signaled that he intended to rely on his domestic anti-inflation

measures to counter the dollar's weakness. "I would empha-
size," he told reporters at the news conference at the Fed,
"that the fundamental solution to instability in foreign-
exchange markets does not lie in intervention."[40]

—

Monday was Columbus Day. Banks in the United States
were closed, but there was immediate reaction around the
world. The price of gold, which had already slipped from its
record high on speculation that the United States would be
bolstering the dollar, fell to $374 an ounce in London. At the
same time, the dollar rose sharply against most European
currencies and the Japanese yen.[41] But bankers and economists, at home and abroad, told reporters the probability of
a deeper recession had increased.

When the American banks opened on Tuesday, interest
rates jumped. The Fed watchers were not quite sure how
high the federal funds rate had moved under the new system. *The Washington Post* said the rate, which had been at 12
percent when the banks closed for the long weekend,
climbed as high as 18 percent that day before settling at 13
percent.[42] *The New York Times* reported a high of 15 percent.[43]
In any case, the commercial banks upped the prime rate—the
interest they charge their best customers—a full percentage
point to 14½ percent.[44] Stock prices dropped sharply and
continued to fall for the next three days, setting off nervous
chatter about the market plunges in 1929 that led to the
Great Depression.

Finally, the market settled down. But interest rates continued to climb with swings of several percentage points a
day for almost two years before peaking in the summer and

latter months of 1981. In June, the federal funds rate hit 19.1 percent. The prime rate rose to 20½ percent in August, and for a moment in December it surged to 21½ percent. The cost of mortgages crested at 18.45 percent in October. People with less than perfect credit were paying even higher rates, as were the multitudes who took out consumer loans or accumulated credit card debt.

Volcker himself was surprised at the heights the rates reached.[45] "I never expected interest rates to go up the way they did, as high as they did," he says. He had hoped his new plan would be so stunning that the very announcement of it would have an immediate impact on the spending behavior of Americans. "We wanted people to sit up and say, 'Oh, now things have changed, interest rates will go down. We'll buy bonds,'" he says. "But they didn't quite do that."

To produce the changes Volcker thought were crucial, Americans had to go through a lot of hard times. The economy slumped sharply in the spring of 1980, and in 1981 and 1982 the country struggled through a recession that drew comparisons to the Great Depression.

Finally, in the summer of 1982, with the nation yearning for relief, Volcker quietly began to loosen his grip on the flow of money. But it was not until the fall that he disclosed signs of a breakthrough. "The forces are there that would push the economy toward recovery," he told a meeting of the Business Council, an organization of America's most influential captains of business and industry, at the elegant Homestead Hotel in Hot Springs, Virginia, in early October.[46] "I would think that the policy objective should be to sustain that recovery," Volcker added.

Alan Greenspan, who later succeeded Volcker as chairman of the Fed and won a degree of acclaim for his confounding talent at circumlocution, that day served as interpreter of Volcker's remarks. "They have eased," said Greenspan, who was attending the meeting as the head of the National Commission on Social Security Reform.[47]

Volcker's strategy seemed to have worked. Unemployment was still above 10 percent, higher than it had been since 1940, and would rise even higher in the next few months. But inflation had been knocked down to an annual rate of 6.5 percent, less than half what it had been two years earlier. Volcker figured he could begin to fuel the economy with a little more money without igniting a new wave of inflation.

But getting to that point had required iron-willed determination. The whole country, it seemed, had been alternately pleading and demanding that Volcker loosen his stranglehold on the economy, with some of the most intense pressure coming from just three blocks away—the White House.

CHAPTER NINE

THE FALLOUT

espite the pain he inflicted on their administrations and the country, Presidents Carter and Reagan rarely criticized Volcker openly, perhaps recognizing that doing so might be interpreted as an attempt to shift blame from their own offices. However, their aides, especially President Reagan's, felt free to take shots at the chairman of the Fed, and they went at him publicly and privately. Unbeknownst to his critics at the time, their greatest achievement was to draw national attention to Volcker, making him one of the best-known Washington leaders—at first reviled as the father of recession, later hailed for fostering prosperity.

Under pressure, Volcker was immovable. He believed in his mission with the fervor of a priest, and he perceived that his critics among the president's legions either did not understand basic economics or were pursuing political objectives that contradicted economics. This unyielding quality might not be ideal in many situations, but the Volcker style had certain advantages if you accepted the argument that the terrible inflation of the late 1970s was in part the result of the unwillingness of previous Fed chairmen to stay the course.

The enduring complaint about Volcker is that he kept interest rates too high for too long, prolonging the 1981–1982 recession at the cost of millions of jobs, with particularly heavy damage to the auto and housing industries. At the annual convention of the National Association of Homebuilders in early 1982, Richard Harwood, a contractor from North Brook, Illinois, told a reporter from *The New York Times* that the focus in his business had become survival.[1] "Everyone used to say, 'How's the family?,'" Harwood said. "Now it's, 'How long do you think you can last? Can you make it through [the year]?'"

Volcker's policies are also widely blamed for contributing to the Latin American debt crisis that began in the summer of 1982 and to the failure of scores of American savings and loan banks later in the decade. In both cases, high interest rates, while not the only factor, were the culprit that forced the issue. Yet Volcker led negotiations that helped Mexico and the other countries get back on their feet, and, for most economists, his reverses were far overshadowed by his defeat of inflation. That victory was "essential to laying the groundwork for the performance of the United States in the 1990s," says Allen Sinai, the founder and chief executive of Decision Economics, a consulting firm in New York.[2]

Warren E. Buffett, the renowned investor and founder and chairman of Berkshire Hathaway, has not always agreed with Volcker's strategies, yet regards him as a giant of finance. "In the seventies the country sort of lost confidence in itself," Buffett says.[3] "People thought that owning land or anything was better than owning dollars and it took a very strong character and a lot of guts to stem that feeling. You had to be smart. But you had to have a lot of guts. It took courage to hang in there and Volcker hung in there."

Like some of his colleagues, Joseph E. Stiglitz, the Columbia University Nobel Prize winner in economics, says Volcker could have employed other tools to bring down inflation and even contends that inflation might have died a natural and rather painless death as America gradually adjusted to the shock of a pair of tremendous surges in oil prices in the 1970s and benefited from later declines in petroleum costs.[4]

But, Stiglitz concedes, it is impossible to know how things would have worked out had Volcker not clamped down. "We can describe the benefit of what he did, which is that he brought down inflation," Stiglitz says. "And we can describe the costs. But we can't know for sure what would have happened if he had tried another approach."

Volcker's special strength in political Washington drew from a single, fundamental desire he felt throughout his life: to seek nothing beyond the freedom to follow his principles. So it was difficult for presidential aides to gain leverage on him. He did not aspire to other jobs in Washington and he was confident that he eventually would be welcomed in private business. He wanted to be respected and liked, but if he was not regularly invited to White House social events, well, he would have to live with that.

Nevertheless, to succeed as chairman of the Fed required sensitive political instincts. Volcker muted his criticism of the presidents and their policies—for which some fellow economists criticized him—and displayed agility in his testimony before Congress. Both Congress and the president had the potential to intervene in his policies, either by law or simple place of power, and as much as neither wanted to do so, it was up to Volcker to make sure that they never felt compelled to permit their objections to go beyond words. So Volcker, like his predecessors at the Fed, tried to avoid confrontation, to accommodate without compromising. One political tactic that came naturally to Volcker was procrastination. "He always had an ability to dominate an issue without using his elbows," a Treasury official, John Auten, told *Newsweek*.[5] "It was based on a great ability to just stand there, doing nothing, until something absolutely had to be done. And then people went to him."

Another tactic, a cousin of procrastination, that especially annoyed more doctrinaire economists, was diffusion. "Someone will accuse the Fed of not paying enough attention to, say, total credit volume and Paul will let it be known, sooner or later, that the Fed is now taking into account total credit volume," said Jude Wanniski, an economic strategist for President Reagan and a frequent critic of Volcker.[6] "And then," Wanniski added in an interview with *Newsweek*, "someone will say, 'You're not paying enough attention to commodity prices.' And he'll make a speech saying, 'Yes, we're paying attention to commodity prices, too.' And then someone will scream, 'But what about Reese's Peanut Butter Cups?' and Paul will say, 'We're now incorporating Reese's Peanut Butter Cups into our view of monetary policy.'"

—

President Carter tried one sharp frontal attack on Volcker, but it backfired, and he soon let it drop. More than 20 years later his criticism seems mild, but at the time it resounded like a hand grenade. In early October 1980, just a month before the presidential election, Carter was feeling edgy, frustrated by an economy that would cause Americans to give the wrong answer when candidate Ronald Reagan later asked, "Are you better off than you were four years ago?" and staring at the growing probability that he was going to be voted out of office. During a campaign stop outside Philadelphia, someone at a small backyard gathering asked about Volcker's emphasis on the money supply in fighting inflation. Carter said he thought it was "ill-advised,"[7] and that the Fed ought to be paying more attention to "the adverse effects of high interest rates on the general economy."[8] Carter's Treasury secretary, G. William Miller, and his chief spokesman, Jody Powell, issued similar complaints, giving the impression of a coordinated assault. It was the administration's first real slap at Volcker since Carter had appointed him a little more than a year earlier, and it immediately drew fire from former Fed chairmen and the Reagan presidential campaign as an affront to the tradition of the Fed as an independent and sacrosanct institution. Arthur F. Burns, Volcker's old friend and colleague at the Fed, called Carter's remarks "regrettable";[9] Burns's predecessor, William McChesney Martin, said the comments were "deplorable" and that Carter had done a "serious and unfortunate thing."[10] Former president Gerald Ford, campaigning for Reagan, called Carter's criticism "a cowardly act,"[11] and George P. Shultz, who was serving as chairman of Reagan's economic policy coordinating committee, elaborated on Ford's remark, chiding Carter for trying to divert responsibility for the ailing economy away from himself.[12] Less than two weeks after his remarks in Philadelphia, President Carter spoke for 20 minutes about the economy in an address to the National Press Club in Washington and never mentioned Volcker.

The economy was only one point of vulnerability for Carter. He suffered tremendously from the takeover of the American embassy in Iran in which more than 50 American diplomats were taken hostage. His inability to gain their release over more than a year added, perhaps unfairly, to his image as an ineffectual leader. Too many Americans concluded that Jimmy Carter just could not get things done. In a poll on election day conducted jointly by the Associated Press and NBC News, two-thirds of the voters said Carter's performance as president was fair or poor.[13]

But the economy was pivotal in Carter's defeat. Shortly after the election, a New York Times/CBS News poll showed that 73 percent of Americans regarded the economy as the country's biggest problem,[14] and the Associated Press/NBC News poll found that on the day Carter was swept from office, voters expressing concern about inflation endorsed Reagan three to one.

Years later, Stuart E. Eizenstat, President Carter's chief domestic adviser, noted Volcker's accomplishment in breaking the back of inflation. But he said Volcker "also broke the back of the Carter administration."[15]

—

While Volcker's high interest rates helped Reagan win the presidential election in 1980, Reagan soon had to learn to live with these rates himself. As he took office the country was heading into the worst recession in decades, and Volcker spoke out relentlessly against the growing budget deficits that resulted from Reagan's tax cuts and defense spending and that most mainstream economists agreed were fueling inflation. In a White House news conference in January 1982, after Reagan had been in office one year, a reporter asked the president if he agreed with those on Capitol Hill who were calling for Volcker's resignation. Reagan was noncommittal, citing the independence of the Fed. "There's no way that I can comment on that," Reagan said.[16]

But a month later, Reagan shifted gears, deciding to embrace Volcker and cast himself as an ally in dealing with the nation's economic problems. Reagan, the old college football player, seemed to have decided that the best offense was a good defense, that publicly aligning himself with Volcker might neutralize the chairman. On February 15th the president invited Volcker to the White House for a private meeting and a few days later voiced his strong support for him. "I have confidence in the announced policies of the Federal Reserve Board," Reagan said in opening remarks at a White House meeting with reporters. "The administration and the Federal Reserve can help bring inflation and interest rates down faster by working together than by working at cross-purposes."[17]

But the president's allies did not relent. Howard Baker, then the majority leader in the Republican-controlled Senate and later Reagan's chief of staff, complained that Volcker's Fed "should get its boot off the neck of the economy."[18] Donald T. Regan, secretary of the Treasury for the first four years of the Reagan administration and then chief of staff for two years, persistently found fault with Volcker. Shortly before Reagan's conciliatory gesture toward Volcker, Regan, a former chief executive of Merrill Lynch, referred to the

Fed chairman as "obstinate and tyrannical,"[19] and in his memoir he mockingly called Volcker a "nanny" who seemed to enjoy correcting bankers "for the sake of correcting."[20] In his book, Regan noted that Volcker's "actions did cauterize inflation" in America, but added that "the burn cost the patient the use of his right arm for nearly two years."

Even with all the derision, by late spring and early summer of 1983, Volcker was beginning to look like a hero. The high interest rates were beginning to pay off. Volcker had beaten down inflation to an annual rate of under 4 percent, from about 13 percent when he took office, and he was loosening up on the money supply. A recovery was under way that would stretch far into the future. Unemployment was still running above 10 percent and would remain a persistent concern, but it was on the way down, and by the end of the year it would be close to 8 percent.

His success notwithstanding, Volcker was still not a favorite of the Reagan administration. His four-year term was expiring in August, but the White House would not say whether he was going to be reappointed. Administration officials told reporters in not-for-attribution conversations that Reagan did not feel he had a good personal relationship with Volcker and some political strategists were recommending that the president replace the Carter appointee with a Republican of his own choice, someone who might be expected to be more supportive at election time. In late April at the annual meeting of the American Newspaper Publishers Association in New York, President Reagan seemed lukewarm to Volcker, despite the president's earlier attempts at cultivating a convivial relationship. He was asked what bothered him about Volcker's performance and responded with three words, "Not a thing,"[21] adding nothing further. That same day, Treasury Secretary Regan took a swipe at Volcker, saying that while the administration had not decided whether to keep him, replacing him would not have the negative impact that some bankers were predicting.[22] In Congress, support for Volcker was mixed. In the Senate, Jake Garns, the Utah Republican and chairman of the Banking Committee, and Senator William Proxmire, the ranking Democrat on the committee, favored another term for Volcker.[23] But in the House, ill feelings toward the chairman had crystallized. Fernand St. Germain, a Democrat from Rhode Island and chairman of the House banking committee, opposed Volcker as a symbol of "high interest rates and recession." St. Germain's Republican colleague, Bob Michel of Illinois, also wanted Volcker replaced.[24]

On a Saturday morning in mid-June, President Reagan ended the speculation about Volcker, playfully announcing his decision during his weekly radio broadcast. "We interrupt this program for a news flash," Reagan said, "I have today asked chairman Paul Volcker to accept reappointment for another term. He's agreed to do so, and I couldn't be more pleased."[25]

In the radio announcement Reagan added the stunning assertion that Volcker was "as dedicated as I am to continuing the fight against inflation."[26] Well, yes, Volcker surely seemed dedicated to fighting inflation. But President Reagan? His administration was continually at odds with Volcker, constantly nagging him to let money flow more easily to speed recovery and, once it was under way, make it more robust; that was the opposite of fighting inflation. The way in which Reagan disclosed Volcker's reappointment was a slight in itself. Traditionally, Reagan invited new appointees to appear at the White House with him in a ceremonial welcoming. For Volcker, there would be no ceremony; he learned of his reappointment in a four-minute phone call[27] from the president to his home in New York an hour before the radio broadcast that Saturday morning and went on about his duties when he returned to Washington.

—

The decision for President Reagan came down to fear, just as it had for President Carter. The White House worried that changing Fed chairmen, no matter who the replacement, would be interpreted as a lack of resolve against inflation. Plenty of evidence confronted the administration. "Wall Street believes that anti-inflation policy is totally embodied in his person," Robert Giordano, a financial analyst at Goldman, Sachs & Co., told *Newsweek* in late May.[28] Charles Brown, the chairman of AT&T, told the magazine: "Everybody is exceptionally pleased with the job Volcker's done on inflation. Very few people would like to see the struggle abandoned."[29] In early June, A.G. Becker Paribas, a Wall Street investment firm, took a poll of institutional investors and economists and, 11 days before President Reagan announced his decision, reported that 77 percent of them believed Volcker was the best man to run the Fed.[30] Treasury Secretary Regan referred to the poll in an interview in *The Washington Post* on June 9, saying, "The financial markets seem to favor him, and want him by an overwhelming majority."[31] In the same article, the *Post* said that Senator Paul Laxalt, a Nevada Republican and President Reagan's closest friend in Congress, appeared to be leaning toward Volcker. "Volcker seems to have a lot of support," Laxalt told the *Post*. "There is concern for making a change at a critical time." Not long after the reappointment announcement, *BusinessWeek* reported that the White House also believed that the mixed attitudes in Congress appeared to have swung more in Volcker's favor.[32]

No alternative for chairman came close to Volcker in international expertise. On how Volcker might affect Reagan's reelection campaign in the following year, Regan and the president's other advisers apparently gambled they would do better with Volcker than with a new chairman. Part of the administration's thinking, *The Washington Post* reported, was that a new Fed chairman might feel compelled to make a show of his independence from the White House.[33] Volcker had more than won his spurs in that regard, and the thinking apparently was that his decisions would predictably be tied to economic logic rather than to ulterior motives. Reagan's team could see the economy was moving in the right direction. Hopefully it would stay on course.

Volcker's confirmation hearing was one of the spectacles of the summer of 1983. The Senate Banking Committee scheduled the event for the caucus room in the Russell Building, the Senate's biggest chamber, and still there was not enough space. People crowded along the walls and in the corners of the ornate room where the Watergate hearings had been conducted. The senators and Volcker talked for nearly four hours, and it was a good day for Volcker. Alan Dixon, a Democrat from Illinois, said he had "profound admiration" for Volcker in an "impossible job";[34] John Heinz, a Republican from Pennsylvania, said, "We're lucky to have you as chairman."[35]

Volcker, sitting at a table covered in green felt and puffing on a cigar, surprised the senators when one of them asked whether he planned to serve out his full four-year term. "I do not feel committed to do so," he replied.[36] He said he planned to stay for at least two years, partly because he believed that the tenure of the Fed chairman and the president should coincide. That way, he said, an incoming president could more easily install a person of his choice instead of having to work with a holdover like himself from a previous administration.

By leaving in two years, Volcker would create an opening at the Fed in August of 1985, so that in less than a year after being sworn in, the winner of the 1984 election could nominate his own Fed chairman. Perhaps not so coincidently, the administration had been floating a story from unidentified sources that Volcker might be willing to step aside in two years. Perhaps Volcker had suggested to the administration that choosing him might not lock them into a four-year term; perhaps the administration thought that by circulating the story it was laying the groundwork for evicting Volcker at a time when his departure might not seem so politically threatening. Those points were never clarified. As it turned out, Reagan was reelected in 1984 and Volcker stayed on. But his performance before the senators that day seemed to be another display of his independent attitude and political canniness.

—

Heading into his second term, Volcker was facing some of the most challenging work of his career. It would not be as dramatic as the initial taming of inflation, but at hand was

178

the more delicate task of keeping inflation in check while permitting the economy to grow. Volcker's efforts were complicated by national budget deficits in the $200 billion range. To make up the budget shortfall, the government borrowed money through the sale of Treasury securities. That put it in competition with American business, which was also a big borrower, and raised the overall demand for money, tending to push up interest rates and stimulate inflation.

Volcker kept urging that the deficit be reduced by raising taxes or reducing spending, neither of which were crowd pleasers, and that irritated the White House. For their part, Reagan administration officials prodded Volcker endlessly to steer the economy in the most politically favorable way for them. The week before Volcker's Senate confirmation hearing, Larry Speakes, Reagan's deputy press secretary, said in a press briefing that the White House "would not like to see interest rates increased."[37] Actually, no one wanted to see interest rates increased. Volcker and most other economists believed that raising rates was not an arbitrary decision, but one that became necessary when inflation threatened. Indeed, there were signs at the time that the Fed was quietly raising rates. Some news reports speculated that the White House had dispatched Speakes with his statement, hoping to plant interest rates squarely on the agenda in Volcker's Senate confirmation, to underscore for the public that Congress, too—not just the president—shared responsibility for the vicissitudes of the economy. If so, it was another case of overkill for the Reagan administration; there was no way that the subject of interest rates was not going to come up at the Volcker hearing, no matter what the White House did.

In his book about Alan Greenspan, Bob Woodward of

The Washington Post gives an example of how pressure was brought to bear on Volcker during the Reagan years. James A. Baker III, the White House chief of staff, invited Volcker to a meeting with the president in the residential quarters in the East Wing in the summer of 1984. It was just the three of them in the downstairs library. Baker turned quickly to the subject of the presidential election coming in the fall. He did not want any increases in interest rates that might hurt Reagan's chances. It was a surprisingly direct message and, according to Woodward, Volcker was taken aback. President Reagan sat there, not moving, not speaking. No one would ever be able to say the president had given the Fed orders. "But the president's presence, sitting there calmly—detached or engaged, no one would ever know for sure, including Baker—gave Baker's words all the weight in the world," Woodward wrote.[38]

Volcker lowered interest rates before the election and Reagan won overwhelmingly. But Volcker says his decision had nothing to do with pressure from the White House. "There were technical reasons," he said in a conversation with me in 2003.[39] Still, his decision was controversial. Other members of the Fed were reluctant to cut the rate. "I had to convince the board to ease," he says. "There was an accusation that I eased despite the board, that I overinterpreted my leeway. I don't think so. But people did say that."

Volcker told Woodward he considered reporting the meeting in the White House library to the Senate Banking Committee, then decided not to. It was perhaps the most blunt attempt to influence him. And, according to Volcker, it was totally unnecessary.

But the Reagan administration did not let up. In the fall

of 1985, the White House offered Volcker the presidency of the World Bank as a graceful way of getting rid of him. A few months later, Volcker was confronted by what he regarded as an attempted coup. Two Reagan appointees had recently joined the seven-member Federal Reserve Board, increasing the number of board members chosen by Reagan to four and giving them a majority. Like the Reagan administration itself, the four Reagan appointees favored looser controls on money. On the morning of February 24, 1986, the four members, including Vice Chairman Preston Martin, who had served as commissioner of savings and loan associations in California when Reagan was governor, argued for easing up on the money supply by lowering the discount rate, the interest rate that the Fed charges banks, to 7 percent from 7½ percent. Volcker wanted to delay. He favored lowering the rate, but he was concerned about setting off a run against the dollar unless the decision was coordinated with Germany and Japan. If interest rates in the United States suddenly dipped below those of the other countries, investors would move out of dollars to take advantage of the higher return on those other currencies. Volcker was in the midst of trying to get Germany and Japan to reduce their interest rates, but had not yet received commitments. Besides the impact on the dollar, an immediate decision in Washington would embarrass Volcker with German and Japanese finance officials.

Martin and the other Reagan appointees insisted on voting. For the first time, Volcker was in the minority, and he left the conference room in a fury. "It was obviously preconceived," Volcker says.[40] "Nobody ever called for a vote suddenly against a chairman when it wasn't even on the agenda."

He left the group with the strong impression that he

intended to resign. The vote was to be made public, as usual, at 4:30 P.M., and Volcker would not accept the public humiliation of having lost control of his board.

Volcker went off to lunch with James Baker, who had shifted from being the White House chief of staff to secretary of the Treasury, and Jesus Silva-Herzog, the finance minister of Mexico. Baker knew an upheaval at the Fed would embarrass the Reagan administration with Wall Street and roil the markets.

In the early afternoon, Volcker met with Wayne Angell, a farmer and former economics professor at Ottawa University in Ottawa, Kansas, and one of the recent Reagan appointees. Preston Martin joined them. Angell and Martin, who insisted publicly that they had not been coached, agreed that the board should reconvene, cancel the vote, and give the chairman time to complete his negotiations with Germany and Japan. The afternoon press release was torn up and Volcker stayed on.

His authority was weakened, but he still controlled the Fed's larger policy-making body, the 12-member Federal Open Market Committee consisting of himself and the six other governors and the presidents of five of the regional Federal Reserve banks. The incident remained secret for about two weeks, until reports of it began to appear in newspapers. A few days after the incident became public, Vice Chairman Preston Martin, who had become Volcker's chief antagonist inside the Fed, resigned. He had hoped to eventually replace Volcker as chairman, and news reports speculated that the White House had told him that was not going to happen.

For Volcker the rebellion was the beginning of the end. The Reagan administration had him outnumbered on his own board, and the sniping from beyond the Fed continued. His second term was due to end in August of 1987.

Over the next year or so, the administration dangled the suggestion that Volcker would be offered another four years interspersed with leaked comments that, of course, he would not. Years later, it is hard to tell what Volcker wanted. His wife was struggling with worsening health problems and the family had been strained by the separation and the big pay cut he had taken as chairman. Balanced against those concerns was Volcker's love of the job.

By some accounts, he agonized over whether to make himself available for another four years. As Bob Woodward tells it, aides to Reagan did not want Volcker to stay on, but were unable to get a clear reading from President Reagan. Reagan himself made no overtures and Volcker was unwilling to coax an invitation from him.

On the afternoon of June 1, 1987, Volcker ended the uncertainty: He was stepping down. He delivered the message personally to President Reagan in the White House. Howard Baker, the chief of staff, and Jim Baker, the secretary of the Treasury, were at the president's side. Reagan did not try to persuade Volcker to stay. As Volcker turned toward the door, he handed Reagan his formal letter of resignation. The chief of staff and the secretary of the Treasury had already lined up Alan Greenspan, a New York Republican who ran his own economic consulting firm, had served as the chairman of the Council of Economic Advisers under Presidents Nixon and Ford, and frequently appeared on television and before Congress. Minutes after Volcker left the White House, President Reagan phoned Greenspan to tell him the job was his. The Volcker era was over.

CHAPTER TEN

FLY-FISHING

Coming out of his high-profile post as chairman of the Federal Reserve for eight years, with commentators often referring to him as the second most powerful person in America, Paul Volcker was a dream prospect for corporate America. The gilded doors of Wall Street swung open to him as if he were a prince. Volcker had none of the riches or even the most visible mannerisms of the clients or the financiers of Wall Street, but the attraction among potential employers lay in a deep sense that the mere association of his name with a financial enterprise would lift its prospects.

Volcker was the stiff, inflexible man of integrity, deliberately unfashionable and irascibly honest as he had always been. Somehow, get Volcker on your team and money would come. They believed that on Wall Street and it proved to be true. For his outwardly humble part, Volcker could surely stand a raise from the $89,500 he earned in his last year at the Fed. He had almost no money; one report put his personal savings at $62,000[1] if you didn't count his rambling Upper East Side apartment. But Volcker did not feel a need for an enormous amount of money. He was not dreaming of mansions and limousines and personal tennis courts, and that made it especially hard for the Wall Street chieftains to win him over. They did not have what he needed.

Seven months after Volcker said goodbye to the Fed, the tall man from Teaneck announced his new place of business. He was not joining one of the giants of finance, but would become chairman of the small investment banking firm, James D. Wolfensohn, Inc. He would also contribute some of what he valued most—his knowledge and experience and sense of decency—to a new generation of students at Princeton University, where he had first felt the spark of excitement that led him into one of the most distinguished careers in economics and public finance.

Volcker did not get into deep discussions with most of the firms that sought his services, but it seemed unlikely that they would feel comfortable about his spending two days a week as the Frederick H. Schultz Class of 1951 Professor of International Economic Policy at Princeton. If they were going to make him a millionaire, they would want all his time. But for James Wolfensohn, Princeton was no problem.

Wolfensohn had left Salomon Brothers as its chief investment banker with the beginnings of a small fortune in 1981 to start his own firm precisely because he wanted the freedom to hone his concert-hall-quality cello skills in his office on any particular afternoon[2] and to devote much of his energy to endeavors like his chairmanship of the John F. Kennedy Center for the Performing Arts in Washington and his campaign to help raise $50 million to restore Carnegie Hall. He encouraged the 20 lawyers, economists, and finance specialists in his firm to take on nonprofit work, and he dedicated 20 percent of the firm's annual profits to charity.[3] Here was a firm that could accommodate and challenge Volcker at the same time.

Wolfensohn structured his small company with an eye toward avoiding the conflicts of interest that were seemingly inevitable for the big investment banks. They made their biggest profits from managing mergers and acquisitions (M&A) and they jumped from deal to deal to keep the cash register ringing. That meant that on one transaction, the bank might be representing General Motors, and on the next it might be sitting across the table with a competing carmaker, armed with a ton of inside knowledge about General Motors. The big investment banks also made money by issuing new stocks and bonds for corporations; they bought and sold stocks and bonds for their own accounts as well. The big firms often used those transactions as a way of favoring particular chief executives as an enticement to hand over their lucrative mergers and acquisitions business.

Wolfensohn's firm did not underwrite new issues of stocks and bonds. It did not try to boost earnings by playing the markets. Instead, the firm made a fetish of long-term relationships with clients. The client paid an annual retainer—at one point reportedly $250,000 a year[4]—and the firm worked alongside the chief executive and his own finance team, offering the advice and guidance of a detached expert. When there was an M&A deal to be done, Wolfensohn's firm was there to help make it happen for the customary extra fee. But often the firm would argue against a client's takeover plan and its own opportunity for juicy fees.[5] Integrity like that was directly in line with Volcker's nature.

"We were an inside adviser, not someone just coming along and trying to do a deal," says founder James Wolfensohn.[6] The Wolfensohn bankers saw themselves as objective members of a client's family council. "The idea was to be part and parcel of these firms, to be able to stand back and to try to serve with sufficient continuity so that we had depth of knowledge of the strategic and financial challenges they were facing," says Jeffrey A. Goldstein, who eventually became a vice chairman at Wolfensohn.[7]

Wolfensohn also took the long view on the pay of its own professionals. "The firm did not compensate people based upon the number of transactions they did," Goldstein says.[8] "There was no imbedded incentive to try to generate revenues because of personal interest. We all basically shared in the overall profitability of the firm." The arrangement appealed to companies like American Express, DaimlerBenz, and the Hong Kong and Shanghai Banking Corporation, now known as HSBC, all of which became Wolfensohn clients.

Wolfensohn was just what Volcker wanted. "You were an adviser to a firm in a confidential way over a period of time," he says.[9] "If they did mergers and acquisitions, you worked on that. But you weren't dependent upon that. You were there, all the time, as a resource. You were unconflicted because that was all we did. No trading. No financing. No nothing. We were there to give unbiased, unconflicted, sound advice. This was our schtick. It was a good schtick. That's why I went there."

Size had been a factor as well. As unlikely as it might seem, Volcker actually saw himself getting lost in a big firm. "The problem at many of these places," he told James Sterngold of *The New York Times*,[10] "was that the firm would go on pretty much as it was, whether I was there or not."

Volcker had other reasons, too. "I didn't want to work for anybody anyway," he said. "I didn't want to be a subordinate. And I didn't want to be the umpteenth consultant they had."[11] Volcker had been telling family and friends that he especially did not want to become a highly paid glad-hander, a rainmaker, the big name that draws business to a firm but may spend little time on substantive matters.[12] That was another attraction of Wolfensohn for Volcker. "We didn't go out hustling for business," Wolfensohn says. "All our business came to us by referrals, one client to the other."[13]

Wolfensohn and Volcker had known each other for nearly a decade. They had met in 1979 in the government-led effort to head off the bankruptcy of the Chrysler Corporation.[14] After Congress agreed to guarantee $1.5 billion in private loans, Wolfensohn, as the head investment banker at Salomon Brothers and as Chrysler's outside financial adviser, cajoled the country's reluctant banks to put up the money under terms they regarded as too favorable to the automaker.[15] Volcker, as the newly arrived chairman of the Federal Reserve, headed the government's Chrysler Loan Guaranty Board, which monitored the deal. "We reported to him all the time on what we were doing in the Chrysler reorganization," Wolfensohn says.[16]

They became friends, and when Volcker announced he was leaving the Fed, Wolfensohn phoned him. "I said, 'I know you're going to get offers from everybody,'" Wolfensohn

recalls, "'but if you want the option of retaining your pri-
vacy, and to give honest advice and do it in a totally professional and noncommercial way, maybe you'd like to come
with me and be chairman.'"[17]

Although Volcker and Wolfensohn came together on the
high plain of ethics, they were very different people. As
Volcker joined the firm, Wolfensohn, who was born in Australia, was building a personal fortune. A one-time basketball
hopeful at Princeton, Volcker had become a sports spectator.
But Wolfensohn, at 53, seven years younger than his new
partner, was still working up a sweat. Wolfensohn had been
on Australia's Olympic fencing team and still played a sharp
game of tennis. He collected art, took his cello most seriously,
and would eventually own his own private jet and four
homes, including a showpiece on 100 forested acres over-
looking the Snake River near Jackson Hole, Wyoming.[18]
Volcker would never be fabulously rich, nor did he aspire to
be. But late in life he was wealthy enough to donate $1.5 mil-
lion to the New York Hospital for Special Surgery to create a
research unit in memory of his wife and an additional
$600,000 to the Rand Institute in California to support work
toward making public service more attractive.

Neither Volcker nor Wolfensohn was willing to disclose
Volcker's starting pay, but as Volcker joined the firm, *The
Washington Post* said people on Wall Street assumed he would
receive well over $1 million a year;[19] *The New York Times* sug-
gested Volcker's pay might be at least $2 million.[20] After a bit
of back-and-forth in an interview with me, Volcker acknowledged that the newspaper estimates were "probably true."[21] In
any case, his pay most certainly rose as the firm grew; the
contrast to his government earnings was staggering. But the

newfound money did not change Volcker's lifestyle. Toward the end of his first year at Wolfensohn, he told *Forbes* magazine the main difference was that instead of just keeping ahead of his family's expenses he was now socking money away.[22]

—

As a professor at Princeton, Volcker would usually drive out of New York across the Hudson River and down to the campus on Friday evenings in the fall and spring in a chauffeured sedan[23] with his wife, Barbara, have a quiet weekend in the pre-Revolutionary home that the university provided, then teach on Mondays and Tuesdays.[24]

He taught graduate and undergraduate students at the Woodrow Wilson School of Public and International Affairs, often bringing in well-known friends as guest lecturers. In his first semester in the fall of 1988, he asked his undergraduate students to write a term paper on "How to Reform the Ailing Federal Deposit Insurance System."[25]

In 1992, one of Volcker's graduate seminars at Princeton was published as a book that covered the highlights of his government career and was as close as he ever came to writing an autobiography.[26] He shared the seminar with Toyoo Gyohten, a career official in the Ministry of Finance of Japan. Gyohten's lectures were published as alternating chapters in the book, giving the Japanese perspective on Volcker's version of events.[27]

To accommodate Barbara Volcker's decreasing mobility, Princeton modified Volcker's campus home, installing a ground floor bedroom and bathroom. But the commute of an hour or so each way to Princeton and the need to navigate steps and other ordinary obstacles that the able-bodied scarcely think about became too much for Volcker's wife. At the same time, Volcker found himself more fully occupied with his duties at Wolfensohn. So, about five years after it had begun, his life as an academic ended. "The single most important factor probably was that Barbara got sick enough so that she couldn't go to Princeton," Volcker says. "And at that point it just lost its appeal. I spent progressively less time; partly it was supply and demand. I didn't want to go down there because she couldn't go and meanwhile you get more involved in the business."[28]

——

For years, Wolfensohn had coveted the presidency of the World Bank. In 1995, President Bill Clinton nominated him for the post, and the bank's directors quickly voted to confirm him. With Wolfensohn's departure, Volcker became the chief executive of the firm.

It had been seven years since he had joined Wolfensohn in 1988, and in that time the firm had greatly expanded. The Chase Manhattan Bank, where Volcker had worked early in his career and where Wolfensohn also had close ties, was one of many new clients. When Volcker first joined the firm, he was Wolfensohn's only partner; now in 1995 there were 10 partners and a total of 140 employees, up from 50, and 50 clients where there had been only a dozen. At Wolfensohn's behest, Volcker oversaw the start-up of joint ventures with the Fuji Bank in Tokyo[29] and J. Rothschild & Company in London,[30] designed to assist Japanese and European companies in business dealings in the United States and American companies in ventures in

Asia and Europe. Volcker had clearly proven his worth. "He added tremendously to the firm," Wolfensohn says.[31]

In 1995, a huge scandal began unfolding at the Bankers Trust New York Corporation, one of the country's biggest banks. The bank specialized in racy derivatives, custom-tailored financial instruments that, as the name implies, derive their value from underlying stocks, bonds, currency, commodities, and financial indexes. Some of the bank's clients, including Procter & Gamble, filed lawsuits to recover tens of millions in derivatives losses. And, in the course of the litigation, a tape recording turned up of Bankers Trust traders laughing about taking advantage of clients who did not seem to understand how derivatives worked.[32] Bankers Trust eventually paid federal regulators $10 million to settle fraud charges and the chief executive resigned.[33]

In January of 1996, Frank N. Newman, fresh from duty as a deputy secretary of the Treasury, took charge of Bankers Trust. Job One for him was cleaning up the bank's reputation. His thoughts soon turned to Wolfensohn, the home of Paul Volcker, and a possible merger as a way to jump-start his revamping of Bankers Trust's image.

Volcker and Newman had met years earlier when Volcker was chairman of the Fed and Newman was the chief financial officer of BankAmerica Corporation. "When I started at Bankers Trust, Paul and I got together for lunch," Newman told Saul Hansell of *The New York Times*. "It was social at first, but then we started to talk about how our two firms could work together."[34]

Volcker and his partners had turned down several previous opportunities to sell their firm.[35] "I thought we had a nice little firm," Volcker says.[36] But he and his partners liked Newman and his plans to restore Bankers Trust's good name.[37] Some of the partners saw a merger with Bankers Trust as a chance to expand their already extensive international business through the bank's network of offices in Europe, Asia, and Latin America.[38] Volcker had felt a tension between the partners who wanted a bigger Wolfensohn, with more opportunities for increased wealth, and others like himself, who valued a smaller firm. Some partners were also apparently impressed that Newman was willing to pay $210 million for their firm, as much as 40 percent more than some analysts expected it to fetch.

Newman announced the acquisition of Wolfensohn on May 22, 1996. No purchase price was disclosed, but financial analysts estimated it at $150 million. A month later, the bank disclosed in documents filed with the Securities and Exchange Commission that it had paid $210 million, almost entirely in stock.[39] Analysts commented that drawing the Wolfensohn firm and Volcker into its fold gave the bank "instant credibility."[40] Saul Hansell of *The New York Times* said the connection with Volcker "was a much-needed infusion of integrity" for Bankers Trust.[41]

Wolfensohn, as the founder of the firm, received the greatest portion of the proceeds, which *The Guardian* estimated at $60 million.[42] Volcker and the nine other partners divided what remained. Had they taken equal shares, Volcker would have presumably received at least $15 million. He will not say how much his share came to, but he says he and some other senior partners received larger portions than the others based on the percentage of their ownership in the firm.[43] In any case, it's safe to say that Volcker made much more in one day than he'd earned in 30 years of government service. Yet he was still far from rich by Wall Street standards, where by the end of 2003 some chief executives were being paid more than $15 million a year and others even boasted fortunes in the billions.

For Volcker, the sale of Wolfensohn was the end of his investment banking career. While his nine partners became executives of Bankers Trust and of its new unit, BT Wolfensohn M&A and Corporate Advisory Group, Volcker resigned from day-to-day responsibilities. As part of the deal, he reluctantly became a director of Bankers Trust, raising its board membership to 13. Even with Frank Newman at the helm and the bank avowedly following a new, clean path, Volcker felt uneasy about being associated with it. Plenty of people, he feared, still associated Banker's Trust with the unethical behavior that Newman had been hired to expunge. "The bank was well known as being very aggressive in those days," Volcker says.[44]

Leaving investment banking did not mean Volcker was heading out to pasture. In August of 1996, as the details of the sale of Wolfensohn were being tied up, Volcker held his first meeting as chairman of the committee that investigated the Swiss bank accounts of the Holocaust victims. He was also on the board of the American Stock Exchange, United Airlines, Nestlé, and the Prudential Insurance Company of America. Since 1991, he had been the North American chairman of the Trilateral Commission, the controversial organization founded by David Rockefeller and comprising mainly business and academic leaders from North America, Europe, and Japan. He was also the chairman of the Group of 30, a private research organization of some of the world's most distinguished economists, central bankers, and bank executives. And in 1998 and 1999 he returned to teaching as a visiting professor at the Stern School of Business at New York University.

—

For Paul Volcker, nothing came close to the magnetic pull of his work in economics, finance, and international affairs. But when he wanted to take a break, he most often went fishing. Volcker is a fly-fisherman, the most elegant, refined, and erudite form of angler. Fly-fishing takes patience and determination and is something of a metaphor for Volcker's life in finance.

It takes fine timing and agility and an understanding of how the waters are moving and how the fish are feeding, not nearly as serious but not all that far removed from the concept of market analysis. Yet, it is hard to think of anything in finance, however exquisite the formulation, that comes close to the beauty of a fly line curling and elongating over a fisherman's head in the poetic and glorious ballet of the cast. Volcker and friends who have shared a stream with him say his form is not great. But, partly aided by his height, he can cast a tiny fly in a soaring arc of 80 or 90 feet, much farther than most people.

Volcker goes after the most difficult fish. No one says it is easy to coax a trout to take a fly, but the fishing is even more challenging with his favorites: Atlantic salmon, bonefish, and tarpon.

Fly-fishing requires intelligence, stamina, and great perseverance, and it benefits from a childlike belief that if you just keep trying you will ultimately succeed in finding a way to get the fish to come to the hook, then sufficiently exhaust itself so that it cannot possibly break the line and defeat its antagonist. That was exactly the Volcker that America saw at the helm of the Federal Reserve. Other chairmen had tried to stop inflation, but their resolve drifted and the inflation monster breathed fire back at them. Volcker stayed with it. Eventually, inflation crumbled.

Volcker has no patience for self-analysis—at least not in public—and he would never acknowledge reading much into his love of fishing. But the traits that have worked for him in fly-fishing were crucial assets in his battle against inflation. E. Gerald Corrigan spent much of his life working in the Federal Reserve system, some of the time as a close aide and fishing buddy of Volcker, and he sees the art of fly-fishing as closely related to the art of central banking. "You have to be very disciplined, very precise, totally focused," Corrigan said one day at his office in the Wall Street district at Goldman Sachs, where he is a managing director. "The concentration is unbelievable."[45]

Corrigan, who served as president of the Federal Reserve banks in Minneapolis and New York, learned fly-fishing from Volcker. His luck was immediately good. The first time out in Montana, he caught a bigger trout than the master; a year later, fishing again with Volcker, he hauled in an even bigger fish. Working a trout stream, Corrigan says, the fly-fisherman "has to get the fly to float down the river exactly at the same speed as the current, or the fish will notice the fly is not real."

"And when the fish rises to take the fly," he continues, "you have an absolute millisecond to strike—or the fish is gone."[46]

Volcker had more than a millisecond to make the critical

move in his fight against inflation—the decision to focus on the supply of money in the United States economy rather than following tradition and adjusting interest rates. But he believed he was working with a narrow window of opportunity and he struck decisively. Then, as interest rates soared and the pain of many Americans increased, Volcker held firm.

That is the way he fishes. "He perseveres," says Bob Wilson, a former vice chairman of Johnson & Johnson, who has fished with Volcker for 15 years.[47] "He knows you've got to keep at it."

EPILOGUE

A s important as fishing has been to Volcker, it has been out there on the margins of his life, a fascinating way to escape into the wilds, but not even a close competitor with the give and take of finance, economics, and international relations.

Most days, Volcker is in his office in Rockefeller Center by 10:00 A.M., writing speeches in longhand on a yellow legal pad, dealing with the handful of clients he advises, the Holocaust settlement, and a dozen or so nonprofit organizations such as the International Accounting Standards Board, the Group of 30, and the Japan Society. He keeps two secretaries busy and seldom leaves the office before 6:00 or 7:00 in the evening.

Two or three nights a week he goes straight to a business dinner. At lunch, for efficiency's sake, he prefers a bowl of soup at his desk. But a couple of days a week, if someone else is paying, he will dart down to the Sea Grill restaurant, which looks out through floor-to-ceiling windows at the

Rockefeller Center ice skating rink, or drop into an Italian restaurant just across the street from his office.[1]

Volcker likes the road. Almost every week he is off to somewhere. For example, on the morning of October 2, 2003, a Thursday, he flew to Washington to testify before a Senate committee, then drove to Shenandoah University in Winchester, Virginia, with Joseph Coyne, his former spokesman from his days at the Federal Reserve. At the university, he delivered a speech and received yet another honorary doctorate. (He has been awarded more than 50 honorary degrees, including three from his alma maters: Princeton, Harvard, and the London School of Economics.) The next day, Volcker flew to Syracuse, New York, for a meeting of the advisory board of the Maxwell School of Public Administration at Syracuse University and to deliver another speech.[2]

Two or three times a year, he tears off on a marathon journey with several overnight legs followed by early morning meetings. On a trip in the fall of 2003, he hit five cities in four countries in 13 days with plane changes in three other cities in Europe and Asia. He did not seem to realize that he was 76 years old.

The expedition in October began with a flight to Washington for a meeting with a senator that was canceled while Volcker was en route. That afternoon, October 28, a Tuesday, he spoke on a panel dealing with the federal budget. Then, at 10:00 that evening, he caught a plane to Frankfurt. He arrived in Germany the next morning at 11:35 A.M., and, after two hours in the airport, continued on to Moscow. In three days in Moscow, he spent a day in meetings preparing to run a five-hour session of the International Accounting Standards Board, lectured for two hours to students at a high school specializing in economics, then moved on to meetings at the Russian central bank, congress, and the offices of the United States Agency for International Development.

It went on like that for almost two weeks, with stops of a few days also in Brussels, Hong Kong, and Beijing. En route to Hong Kong, Volcker finished running an all-day meeting of his international accounting board in Brussels and caught a 6:00 P.M. flight to London to make a connection to Asia. He arrived in Hong Kong at 6:00 P.M. the next day, just in time to get to a dinner given by C. H. Tung, the chief executive of the city. At 8:00 the next morning, Volcker and others on Tung's international advisory council started a day of meetings. At 7:00 P.M. Volcker flew to Beijing.

He got back to New York, on a flight from Beijing via Tokyo, as darkness was falling on Sunday, November 10. On Monday, he was in his office by about 10:00 A.M. as usual. I dropped by to talk with him Tuesday morning. Sipping black coffee and tilting back jauntily in his high-backed leather armchair, he looked like he'd just come off a vacation.

Volcker will speak to almost any university or professional group that offers him a platform for his favorite themes: careers in public service, honest accounting, central banking, international trade, the general drift of the economy. Most of the time, he speaks for free. "You're educating people," Volcker says.[3] "They ought to hear what's right and what's wrong about American business."

For about a half dozen speeches a year he collects a fee in the tens of thousands of dollars. With two or three speeches, he can make more than he was paid annually at the Fed.[4]

In his speeches, Volcker does not tell war stories about

his adventures at the Treasury Department and the Federal Reserve, which would actually make pretty good listening. But Volcker is not dwelling on the past. He is focused on current events and on tomorrow, which, as he sees it, could be immensely better with a reformed civil service and honest accounting.

Not long after leaving government service in Washington, Volcker sat for a long interview with a writer for *The Region,* the magazine of the Federal Reserve bank of Minneapolis.[5] Volcker does not usually respond well to questions aimed at revealing his inner self. But that day, with just a little prompting, one of the great financial strategists and moral leaders quickly fashioned a concise self-portrait.

He began with a touch of diffidence that can make him seem slightly vulnerable and more appealing, but which fades when he has settled on a decision. He said he considered himself discreet—to a fault, some might say—and pragmatic. Then he talked about the way he works and, in a few words, he captured the Paul Volcker that the world has been seeing for decades. "I try to find a consensus solution or a way for people who may disagree to proceed," Volcker said. "But I also think [that] on some basic points, you'd better not be a compromiser."

Bibliography

Authers, John and Wolffe, Richard, *The Victim's Fortune: Inside the Epic Battle over the Debts of the Holocaust* (New York: Harper-Collins, 2002).

Bazyler, Michael J., *Holocaust Justice: The Battle for Restitution in America's Courts* (New York: New York University Press, 2003).

Biven, W. Carl, *Jimmy Carter's Economy: Policy in an Age of Limits* (Chapel Hill: University of North Carolina Press, 2002).

Dahrendorf, Ralf, *LSE: A History of the London School of Economics and Political Science, 1895–1995* (Oxford: Oxford University Press, 1995).

Deane, Majorie and Pringle, Robert, *The Central Banks* (New York: Penguin, 1994).

Eizenstat, Stuart E., *Imperfect Justice, Looted Assets, Slave Labor, and the Unfinished Business of World War II* (New York: Public Affairs, 2003).

Galbraith, John Kenneth, *Money: Whence It Came, Where It Went* (Boston: Houghton Mifflin, 1975).

Greider, William, *Secrets of the Temple: How the Federal Reserve Runs the Country* (New York: Simon & Schuster, 1987).

Hall, Frank (editor-in-chief), *The Teaneck 100 Year Book: Celebrating the Teaneck, New Jersey Centenial, 1895–1995* (Teaneck, NJ: Centennial Committee, Township of Teaneck, 1995).

Heilbroner, Robert L. and Thurow, Lester C., *Five Economic Challenges* (Englewood Cliffs, NJ: Prentice Hall,1981).

Jessurun, Walter S., *Twelve Years: A True Story of Years of Struggle to Make and Keep TEANECK the Ideal Community* (Teaneck, NJ: Teaneck Taxpayers League, 1941). Available at www.

Teaneck.org/virtualvillage/teaneck12years/index.htm under the title *Teaneck's Most Progressive 12 Years: A Success Story to Make and Keep Teaneck the Ideal Community*.

Kettl, Donald F., *Leadership at the Fed* (New Haven, CT: Yale University Press, 1986).

Martin, Justin, *Greenspan: The Man Behind Money* (Cambridge, MA: Perseus, 2000).

Mayer, Martin, *The Fate of The Dollar* (New York: Signet, 1981).

Mayer, Martin, *The Fed: The Inside Story of How the World's Most Powerful Financial Institution Drives the Markets* (New York: Free Press, 2001).

Melton, William C., *Inside the Fed: Making Monetary Policy* (Homewood, IL: Dow Jones-Irwin, 1985).

Morrill, Robert N., *A Glimpse of the Old Days of Teaneck* (Wolfeboro, NH, Kingswood,1982).

Neikirk, William R., *Volcker: Portrait of the Money Man* (New York and Chicago: Congdon & Weed, Inc., 1987).

Nocera, Joseph, *A Piece of the* Action: *How the Middle Class Joined the Money Class* (New York: Simon & Schuster, 1994).

Regan, Donald T., *For the Record: From Wall Street to Washington* (New York: Harcourt Brace Jovanovich, 1988).

Reston, James Jr., *The Lone Star: The Life of John Connally* (New York: Harper & Row, 1989).

Rockefeller, David, *David Rockefeller: Memoirs* (New York: Random House, 2002).

Root, Robert K., *The Princeton Campus in World War II* (Princeton, NJ: bound typed manuscript, 1950).

Schapiro, Jane, *Inside a Class Action: The Holocaust and the Swiss Banks* (Madison, WI: University of Wisconsin Press, 2003).

Solomon, Robert, *The International Monetary System, 1945–1976* (New York: Harper & Row, 1977).

Sprague, Irvine H., *Bailout: An Insider's Account of Bank Failures and Rescues* (New York: Basic Books, 1986).

BIBLIOGRAPHY

Stein, Herbert, *Presidential Economics: The Making of Economic Policy from Roosevelt to Reagan and Beyond* (New York: Simon & Schuster, 1984).

Stiglitz, Joseph E., *The Roaring Nineties: A New History of the World's Most Prosperous Decade* (New York: W. W. Norton, 2003).

Taylor, Mildred, *The History of Teaneck* (Teaneck, NJ: Teaneck American Revolution Bicentennial Committee, 1977).

Wanniski, Jude, *The Way the World Works* (Washington, DC: Regnery Publishing, 4th ed., 1998).

White, Theodore H., *America in Search of Itself: The Making of the President, 1956–1980* (New York: Harper & Row, 1982).

Notes

1. A Finance Legend

1. Transcript of testimony, House of Representatives, Committee on Banking, Finance and Urban Affairs, Washington, DC, July 21, 1981, 224 pages.
2. Paul A. Volcker Jr. interview, 2003.
3. Clyde H. Farnsworth, "Volcker Sees More Tightening," *The New York Times,* July 22, 1981, p. D1.
4. John M. Berry, "Banking Panel Attacks Volcker on Tight Money; Fed Chairman Volcker Attacked on Policies," *The Washington Post,* July 22, 1981, p. E1.
5. Craig T. Ferris, "Volcker Testifies: Fed to Increase Grip on Money, Credit Growth," *The Bond Buyer,* July 22, 1981, p. 1. See also Denis G. Gulino, United Press International, "Inflation: Weaker but Still Threatening," Washington, Saturday, July 25, 1981, AM cycle.
6. Jay Rosenstein, "Federal Reserve Head Draws Fire in Congress over Monetary Policies," *The American Banker,* July 22, 1981, p. 1.
7. Ferris, "Volcker Testifies."
8. George J. Church, "Paying More for Money," *Time,* March 8, 1982, p. 74, reported by David Beckwith and Gisela Bolte with assistance from other bureaus of the magazine around the country.
9. "Threat to Fed Blamed on High Interest Rates," Associated Press, Washington, Monday, December 7, 1981, AM cycle. See also "Economy on His Mind; Man Seized at Federal

Reserve," *The Washington Post*, December 8, 1981, p. B7; United Press International, Washington, Tuesday, December 8, 1981, PM cycle.

10. Bob Woodward, *Maestro: Greenspan's Fed and the American Boom* (New York: Simon & Schuster, 2000), p. 24.
11. Alan S. Blinder interview, 2003.
12. Alan Greenspan interview, 2004.
13. Joseph E. Stiglitz interview, 2003.
14. Alan S. Blinder interview, 2003.
15. Paul A. Volcker Jr. interview, 2003.
16. Alan Greenspan interview, 2004.
17. Henry Kaufman interview, 2003.
18. Paul A. Volcker Jr. interview, 2003.
19. Ibid.

2. Seventy-Six

1. Alan S. Blinder interview, 2003.
2. For detailed, exceptionally readable accounts of Andersen and its problems, see Kurt Eichenwald, "Enron's Many Strands: The Accountants; Miscues, Missteps and the Fall of Andersen," *The New York Times*, May 8, 2002, p. A1C.; Kurt Eichenwald, "Andersen Misread Depths of the Government's Anger," *The New York Times*, March 18, 2002, p. A1; and a series of four articles in the *Chicago Tribune* beginning on September 1, 2002 on the front page under the headline, "The Fall of Andersen: Greed Tarnished Golden Reputation; In Its Drive to Boost Profits, the Chicago Auditing Legend Diluted Its Lofty Standards, Rewarding Partners Who Generated Hefty Consulting Fees and Forcing out Its Blunt Doorkeepers." The series was reported by Delroy Alexander, Greg Burns, Robert Manor, Flynn McRoberts, and E. A. Torriero. It was written by Flynn McRoberts.

3. Delroy Alexander, Greg Burns, Robert Manor, Flynn McRoberts, and E. A. Torriero, *Chicago Tribune*, third of four-part series, September 3, 2002, p. 1.
4. Paul A. Volcker Jr. interview, 2003.
5. Ibid.
6. Arthur Andersen press release, February 3, 2003, issued in Chicago.
7. Jonathan D. Glater, "Enron's Many Strands: The Auditors; Former Fed Chief Picked to Oversee Audit of Enron," *The New York Times,* February 4, 2003, p. A1.
8. Ibid.
9. Ibid.
10. Paul A. Volcker Jr. interview, 2003.
11. Ibid.
12. Ibid.
13. David S. Hilzenrath, "Panel Tells Andersen to Split Its Services; Volcker Board Hopes Industry Will Follow Suit," *The Washington Post,* March 12, 2002, p. E1. See also Cassell Bryan-Low and Milo Geyelin, "Volcker Pushes for a Breakup of Andersen," *The Wall Street Journal,* March 12, 2002, p. C1.
14. Ibid.
15. Hilzenrath, "Panel Tells Andersen to Split Its Services."
16. Bryan-Low and Geyelin, "Volcker Pushes for a Breakup of Andersen."
17. Formal statement of Volcker's Independent Oversight Board, "Volcker Outlines Framework for a 'New Andersen'; With Governing Board, Success Depends on Preconditions Dictated by Market Realities," New York, March 22, 2002.
18. Paul A. Volcker Jr. interview, 2003.
19. Jonathan D. Glater, "Former Fed Chief Outlines Proposal to Save Andersen," *The New York Times,* March 23, 2002, p. A1.
20. David S. Hilzenrath and Susan Schmidt, "Panel Offers to

Lead Andersen; Action Contingent on Dropping of Criminal Charges," *The Washington Post,* March 23, 2002, p. E1.

21. Glater, "Former Fed Chief Outlines Proposal to Save Andersen."

22. Cassell Bryan-Low and Ken Brown, "Andersen: Called to Account; Volcker Steps up as Waste Management Bolts—Ex-Fed Chairman Offers to Take over Andersen amid More Defections," *The Wall Street Journal,* March 25, 2002, p. C1.

23. Eichenwald, "Enron's Many Strands."

24. Paul A. Volcker Jr. interview, 2003.

25. Ibid.

26. Lianne Hart and Jeff Leeds, "Andersen Sentenced to $500,000 Fine, 5 Years of Probation; A Judge Hands out the Maximum Penalty in the Enron-Related Obstruction Case. The Firm Says It's Not Guilty," *Los Angeles Times,* October 16, 2002, p. 3 in the business section.

27. Stephen Labaton, "Volcker Seen as Top Choice to Head Board on Accounting," *The New York Times,* August 23, 2002, p. C1.

28. Christie Harlan, spokeswoman for the Public Company Accounting Oversight Board, interview, 2003.

29. Herb Perone, a spokesman for the Securities and Exchange Commission, interview, 2003. The logic for the high pay, Perone says, is that "if you want to hire people who know the industry and can stand up to the weasels and say, 'Cut that out,' you have to recruit from the very places that the chairman is going to be regulating or supervising." For partners at the big accounting firms, he says, $556,000 is not considered lavish compensation.

30. Paul A. Volcker Jr. interview, 2003.

31. Ibid.

32. Michael Bradfield interview, 2003.

33. Paul A. Volcker Jr. interview, 2003.

34. Ibid.
35. Stuart E. Eizenstat, *Imperfect Justice: Looted Assets, Slave Labor and the Unfinished Business of World War II* (New York: Public Affairs, Perseus Books Group, 2003), p. 71.
36. Ibid., p. 71.
37. Paul A. Volcker Jr. interview, 2003.
38. Ibid.
39. John Authers and Richrd Wolffe, *The Victim's Fortune* (New York: HarperCollins, 2002), p. 26.
40. Michael Bradfield interview, 2003.

3. The Power of the Fed

1. W. Carl Biven, *Jimmy Carter's Economy: Policy in an Age of Limits* (Chapel Hill and London: The University of North Carolina Press, 2002), p. 53 and footnote 65 in Chapter 3, p. 276.
2. Sir Edward George interview, 2002.
3. Anne Poniatowski interview, 2003.
4. Paul A. Volcker Jr. interview, 2003.
5. David Rockefeller interview, 2003.
6. Paul A. Volcker Jr. interview, 2003. See also William R. Neikirk, *Volcker: Portrait of the Money Man* (New York and Chicago: Congdon & Weed, 1987), p. 122.
7. Paul A. Volcker Jr. interview, 2003. See also Neikirk, *Volcker*, p. 122.
8. "The Dollar Chooses a Chairman," *Business Week*, August 6, 1979, Industrial Edition, p. 20.
9. Paul A. Volcker Jr. interview, 2003.
10. David Beckwith, "Paul Volcker: For the Parsimonious Head of the Federal Reserve, Squeezing the Dollar Is Policy, Pinching Pennies a Way of Making Ends Meet," *Time*, May 10, 1982, p. 58.
11. Paul A. Volcker Jr. interview, 2003.

12. John Herbers, "Nixon Picks Simon as Treasury Head but Limits Role," *The New York Times,* April 18, 1974, p. 1.

13. Leonard Sloane, "Volcker to Resign Treasury Job," *The New York Times,* April 9, 1974, p. 55.

14. Paul A. Volcker Jr. interview, 2003.

15. Ibid.

16. Formally, the president of the New York Fed is chosen by the bank's nine-member board and installed with the approval of the chairman of the Federal Reserve Board in Washington and the six other board members. But as one of the most powerful economic officials in the country, the chairman of the Federal Reserve generally gets what he wants within his own system.

17. Neikirk, *Volcker*, p. 159. See also Leonard Sloane, "Volcker to Resign Treasury Job," April, 9, 1974. Sloane reported in a brief story on Volcker's resignation that he had previously been offered the presidencies of the Federal Reserve Banks in Minneapolis and San Francisco and that there was current speculation that he was being considered to head the Federal Reserve Bank in New York. Volcker says that when he resigned from the Treasury Department he did not know where he would work next and that he did not come to terms with Burns until some time later. Then Volcker arranged for a stint of teaching at Princeton.

18. Paul A. Volcker Jr. interview, 2003.

19. Ibid.

20. Peter D. Sternlight interview, 2003.

4. Chairman

1. Robert Solomon interview, 2003.

2. Peter D. Sternlight interview, 2003.

3. Robert Solomon interview, 2003; Peter Sternlight interview, 2003.

4. Stephen H. Axilrod interview, 2003.

5. Ibid.

6. Judith Miller, "Rift over Rates: Miller vs. Blumenthal," *The New York Times,* April 20, 1979, p. D1. See also Judith Miller, "G.N.P. Lags, Inflation Soars–What's an Administration to Do?" April 22, 1979, p. F2.

7. Edward Walsh and Hobart Rowen, "Carter: Oil Rise Makes Recession More Likely; President Sees Recession Risk in OPEC Rise," *The Washington Post,* July 2, 1979, p. A1. See also William H. Jones, "This Spring Most Profitable for Oil Industry: Texaco Earns 132 Percent More During Second Quarter; Oil Industry's Spring Most Profitable," *The Washington Post,* July 27, 1979, p. F1.

8. Fred Barbash and Barry Sussman with contributions from David S. Broder and Valarie Thomas, "The Pessimism: President Facing Growth of Pessimism on Future; Polls Show Growing Doubt about the Future," *The Washington Post,* July 15, 1979, p. A1.

9. Edward Walsh, "Carter Finds 'Crisis of Confidence': Carter Links Energy War to Revival of America's Spirit; 'Energy Will Be the Immediate Test,'" *The Washington Post,* July 16, 1979, p. A1. See also Terence Smith, "A Six-Point Program: President Says Democracy Faces a Severe Threat–Criticism Noted," *The New York Times,* July 16, 1979, p. A1.

10. *The Washington Post,* "Text of President Carter's Address to the Nation," July 16, 1979, p. A14.

11. Martin Schram and Edward Walsh with contributions from David S. Broder, Richard Lyons, Mary Russell, and Ward Sinclair, "Carter Sees Need to Do Better Job, Counter 'Malaise': Carter Wants to Improve His Leadership, Counter 'Malaise'; Camp David Talks Cover Wide Range," *The Washington Post,* July 10, 1979, p. A1, 13. William Safire, "All the Help He Can Get," *The New York Times,* July 12, 1979, p. A21.

12. Safire, "All the Help He Can Get."

13. *The Washington Post,* "Text of President Carter's Address to the Nation."

14. Robert D. Hershey Jr., "Gold Surpasses $300 and Dollar Slumps on Fears about Oil: Possible Carter Cabinet Shift Also a Factor—Blumenthal Cites "Climate of Uncertainty," *The New York Times,* July 19, 1979, p. 1A.

15. Paul A. Volcker Jr. interview, 2003.

16. Ibid.

17. Ibid.

18. Paul Lewis, "Miller Choice Confuses Europe; U.S. Economic Aims Queried," *The New York Times,* July 21, 1979, p. 25.

19. David Rockefeller, *David Rockefeller: Memoirs* (New York: Random House, 2002), p. 369.

20. Terrence Smith, "Hunt For Succesor to Miller Narrows," *The New York Times,* July 25, 1979, p. 1.

21. William R. Neikirk, *Volcker: Portrait of the Money Man* (New York and Chicago: Congdon & Weed, 1987), p. 1–2.

22. Ibid, p. 2.

23. Ibid. p. 2–3.

24. Rockefeller, *Memoirs,* p. 369.

25. William Greider, *Secrets of the Temple: How the Federal Reserve Runs the Country* (New York, Simon & Schuster, 1989), p. 34.

26. Ibid., p. 34.

27. Ibid., p. 35.

28. Paul A. Volcker Jr. interview, 2003.

29. Paul Volcker and Toyoo Gyohten, *Changing Fortunes* (New York: Times Books, 1992), p. 164.

30. W. Carl Biven, *Jimmy Carter's Economy: Policy in an Age of Limits* (Chapel Hill and London: The University of North Carolina Press, 2002), p. 239.

31. Volcker and Gyohten, *Changing Fortunes,* p. 164.

32. Paul A. Volcker Jr. interview, 2003. See also Biven, *Jimmy Carter's Economy,* p. 239. Biven gives Carter's recollection of

the discussion with Volcker concerning the independence of the Fed. "He made it plain," Carter said, referring to Volcker, "and it was mutual, that if he took the job he would want to do it in accordance with my previously expressed policy, that I wouldn't try to put pressure on him or interfere in his best judgment in that important role."

33. Paul A. Volcker Jr. interview, 2003.

34. Greider, *Secrets of the Temple,* p. 47.

35. Ibid., p. 47.

36. Ibid., p. 47.

37. Volcker and Gyohten, *Changing Fortunes,* p. 164.

38. Paul A. Volcker Jr. interview, 2003.

39. Mark Potts, Associated Press, Wednesday, July 25, 1979, AM cycle.

40. Robert A. Bennett, "Nominee Pledges to Fight Inflation and Restore Confidence in Dollar," *The New York Times,* July 26, 1979, p. 1.

41. Lynn Conover, "Volcker Appointment Wins Broad Favor; He Says Fed Will Remain Independent," *The American Banker,* July 26, 1979, p. 1.

42. Greider, *Secrets of the Temple,* p. 47.

43. Associated Press, text of President Carter's news conference, Wednesday, July 25, 1979, BC cycle.

44. James Peltz, Associated Press, coverage of Paul Volcker's New York press conference, Wednesday, July 25, 1979, AM cycle.

45. Ibid.

46. Editorial, "Straight and Narrow with Mr. Volcker," *The New York Times,* July 26, 1979, p. A18.

47. Robert A. Bennett, "Nominee Pledges to Fight Inflation and Restore Confidence in Dollar," *The New York Times,* July 26, 1979, p. A1.

48. Frank Cormier, Associated Press, Washington, Wednesday, July 25, 1979, PM cycle.

49. Transcript of testimony before Senate Committee on Banking, Housing and Urban Affairs on the nomination of Paul A. Volcker to be chairman, Board of Governors, Federal Reserve System, July 30, 1979, 68 pages.

50. Ibid.

51. Senate transcript, July 30, 1979, p. 3. See also Clyde H. Farnsworth, "Volcker Says Jump in Supply of Money Sharpens Inflation: Bid to Cut Growth Is Hinted; Reserve Nominee Stresses Price Stability—Duncan Backed in Senate for Energy Post," *The New York Times,* July 31, 1979, A1; Art Pine, "Volcker Not Sure Recession Here," *The Washington Post,* July 31, 1979, p. D1.g.

52. Ibid.

53. Ibid.

54. Martin Tolchin, "President Pledges to Maintain Course on Economic Policy," *The New York Times,* August 7, 1979, p. A1.

5. Youth

1. Donald W. Maloney interview, 2003.

2. Rabbi Mordecai Weiss, "New Family in the Old Ozzie and Harriet Home," *The Bergen Record,* April 3, 1997, p. 6H.

3. Frank Hall, editor-in-chief, *The Teaneck 100 Year Book* (Teaneck, NJ: Centennial Committee, Township of Teaneck, 1995), p. 29.

4. Paul A. Volcker Sr., typewritten text of retirement speech he gave at the Casa Mana restaurant in Teaneck, NJ on February 18, 1950. He actually stepped down from office later in the year. Teaneck Public Library archives.

5. Paul A. Volcker Jr. interview, 2003.

6. Virginia Volcker Streitfeld interview, 2003.

7. Paul A. Volcker Sr. retirement speech, February 18, 1950.

8. Virginia Volcker Streitfeld interview, 2003.

9. Dick Rodda interview, 2003.

10. Virginia Volcker Streitfeld interview, 2003.

11. Ibid.

12. Ibid.

13. William R. Neikirk, *Volcker: Portrait of the Money Man* (New York and Chicago: Congdon & Weed, 1987), p. 51–52; Paul A. Volcker Jr. and Virginia Volcker Streitfeld interviews, 2003.

14. Neikirk, *Volcker,* p. 51–52.

15. Paul A. Volcker Jr. interview, 2003.

16. Ibid.

17. Ibid.

18. Virginia Volcker Streitfeld interview, 2003.

19. Eric Gelman with Rich Thomas and Nikki Finke Greenberg in Washington and Bill Powell in New York, "America's Money Master," *Newsweek*, February 24, 1986, p. 47.

20. Dorothea Van Duzer interview, 2003.

21. Paul A. Volcker Jr. interview, 2003.

22. Jim Volcker interview, 2003.

23. Virginia Volcker interview, 2003.

24. Neikirk, *Volcker*, p. 51.

25. Dick Rodda interview, 2003.

26. Robert N. Morrill, *A Glimpse of the Old Days of Teaneck* (Wolfeboro, NH: The Kingswood Press, 1982) p. 22.

27. Dick Rodda interview, 2003.

28. Paul Volcker Sr. and his wife, Alma, shared the sense that while they were far from wealthy, there were plenty of others who were less well-off. During the Depression, Mrs. Volcker would not let Paul Jr. and his sisters invite friends over to celebrate their birthdays. "She didn't want other people bringing us presents they might not be able to afford," Virginia Volcker Streitfeld says. "She did not encourage us to babysit because she felt maybe other people needed the money more."

29. Dick Rodda interview, 2003.

30. Virginia Volcker Streitfeld interview, 2003.

31. Jim Volcker interview, 2003.

32. Virginia Volcker Streitfeld interview, 2003.

33. Ibid.

34. Neal Soss interview, 2003.

35. Ernest Patrikis interview, 2002.

36. Bob Henderson, "Scene Here and There," *Teaneck Sunday Sun*, March 20, 1960.

37. Virginia Volcker Streitfeld interview, 2003.

38. Jim Volcker interview, 2003.

39. Helene V. Fall interview, 2003.

40. Frank Hall interview, 2003.

41. Ibid.

42. Paul A. Volcker Sr., typed text of dinner speech marking 25 years as a town manager, beginning in Cape May, NJ. Casa Mana restaurant, Teaneck, NJ, February 18, 1950.

43. Helene V. Fall interview, 2003.

44. Dick Rodda interview, 2003.

45. Virginia Volcker Streitfeld interview, 2003.

46. Ibid.

47. Ibid.

48. Paul A. Volcker Jr. interview, 2003.

6. School Days

1. Paul A. Volcker Jr. interview, 2003.

2. Ibid.

3. Paul A. Volcker Jr. interview, 2002.

4. Ibid.

5. Donald W. Maloney interview, 2003.

6. Ibid.

7. Paul A. Volcker Jr. interview, 2003.

8. Ibid.

9. Ibid.

10. Robert Kavesh interview, 2003.

11. Ibid.

12. Anne Bohm interview, 2002.

13. Paul A. Volcker Jr. interview, 2003.

14. Anne Bohm interview, 2002.

15. Paul A. Volcker Jr. interview, 2003. See also William R. Neikirk, *Volcker: Portrait of the Money Man* (New York and Chicago: Congdon & Weed, 1987), p. 79–80 and 84–85.

16. Paul A. Volcker Jr. interview, 2003.

17. Donald W. Maloney interview, 2003.

18. Neikirk, *Volcker,* p. 116–117.

19. Ibid.

20. Paul A. Volcker Jr. interview, 2003.

21. Ibid.

22. Neikirk, *Volcker*, p. 117.

23. Ibid.

24. Ibid., p. 117.

25. Ibid., p. 117.

26. Ibid, p. 117.

27. Neikirk, *Volcker,* p. 117.

28. Paul A. Volcker Jr. interview, 2003.

29. Neikirk, *Volcker,* p. 117.

7. Hardship

1. Jim Volcker interview, 2003.

2. Ibid.

3. "Behind the 20¢ Cigar," *Time*, March 8, 1982, p. 80–81.

4. Paul A. Volcker Jr. interview, 2003.

5. Jim Volcker interview, 2003.

6. Ibid.

7. Paul A. Volcker Jr. interview, 2003.

8. Ibid.

9. Janice Volcker Zima interview, 2003.

10. Peter Bakstansky, the spokesman for the New York Fed, says the pay for the presidents of the New York bank and other regional banks reflects the prevailing pay levels for bankers in the regions. The boards of the regional banks set the pay for the presidents, he says, at a level they determine is necessary to attract talented people. In contrast, the pay for the chairman of the Federal Reserve follows a federal compensation schedule approved by Congress. In any case, the top salaries throughout the Fed are low in comparison with the pay at big private banks but the prestige of the Fed gives it powerful drawing power. In 2003, the salary of Alan Greenspan, who had been chairman of the Fed since Volcker had stepped down in August 1987, was $171,900. The annual pay for William J. McDonough as president of the New York Fed then was $313,300. McDonough resigned in the summer of 2003 and became the chairman of the Public Company Accounting Oversight Board, a new unit of the Securities and Exchange Commission in Washington.

11. Robert D. Hershey Jr., "Sacrifice a Way of Life for Reserve Chairman," *The New York Times,* June 19, 1983, p. 26.

12. Steven Rattner, "A Look Inside Paul Volcker's Fed," *The New York Times,* May 3, 1981, p. 1, Financial Desk.

13. Christian Zima interview, 2003.

14. "Behind the 20¢ Cigar," p. 80–81.

15. Paul A. Volcker Jr. interview, 2003.

16. Jim Volcker interview, 2003.

17. Most of the 11 million Americans with diabetes in 2003 had Type II or mature-onset diabetes. It is the milder form of the disease and often can be controlled with exercise and diet.

18. Even in 2003, when outcomes had greatly improved, the Joslin Diabetes Center noted in a news release that the risk of birth defects among children of diabetic women was two to

five times higher than for those whose mothers did not have diabetes.

19. Paul A. Volcker Jr. interview, 2003.
20. Ibid.
21. Jim Volcker interview, 2003.
22. Ibid.
23. Ibid.
24. Ibid.
25. Janice Volcker Zima interview, 2003.
26. Christian Zima interview, 2003.
27. Janice Volcker Zima interview, 2003.
28. Ibid.
29. Jim Volcker interview, 2003.
30. Paul A. Volcker Jr. interview, 2003.
31. Janice Volcker Zima interview, 2003.
32. Jim Volcker interview, 2003.
33. Ibid.
34. Dr. William Bahnson interview, 2003.
35. Janice Volcker Zima interview, 2003.
36. Paul A. Volcker Jr. interview, 2003.
37. Christine Godek, director of public relations, Hospital for Special Surgery, e-mail on September 26, 2003.

8. Difficult Choices

1. See editorial, "Matters of Interest," *The Washington Post,* September 8, 1979, p. A14. "A mortgage rate of 12 percent seems fearfully high," the *Post* editorial said. "But if the house keeps appreciating at 12 percent for the life of the mortgage, the real interest is zero and the loan is free. After 15 years' experience with progressively higher inflation rates, Americans are now routinely thinking and working in these terms. High interest rates have lost their shock value." In a similar vein, see also

John Cunniff, AP business analyst, Wednesday, August 8, 1979, PM cycle. Cunniff reported that consumer installment credit in June 1979 shot up to $292.48 billion, 17.1 percent higher than the same month a year earlier, while at the same time workers' take-home pay was being eroded by inflation, falling 3.3 percent in the month of May alone. "Many Americans," Cunniff wrote, "resorted to a well-known but once scorned technique for raising money: They let inflation finance them. They remortgaged their homes and used the money so raised to buy consumer goods." Cunniff said Morgan Guaranty Trust estimated that in each of the two previous years homeowners had borrowed $50 billion through refinancing as the market value of their homes rose. Cunniff quoted G. William Miller, the secretary of the Treasury and former chairman of the Fed, as saying, "If it [inflation] is not checked, then it will threaten our democratic system itself."

2. Paul A. Volcker Jr. interview, 2003.

3. Karen W. Arenson, "Reserve Raises Loan Rate to Banks to Record 10½% from 10% Level," *The New York Times,* August 17, 1979, p. A1.

4. Edward Cowan, "High-Interest Foes Fear Deeper Slump," *The New York Times,* September 20, 1979, p. 1.

5. Robert Parry, Associated Press, Washington, Wednesday, September 5, 1979, PM cycle. See also, "Required Reading," *The American Banker,* September 10, 1979, p. 4, text of prepared statement of Paul A. Volcker Jr., presented at hearing of the of the House Budget Committee, September 5, 1979.

6. John M. Berry, "Fed Lifts Discount Rate to Peak 11% on Close Vote; Fed Increases Discount Rate to Record 11%," *The Washington Post,* September 19, 1979, p. A1.

7. Paul A. Volcker Jr. interview, 2003.

8. Ibid.

9. Ibid.

10. Ibid.

11. Stephen H. Axilrod interview, 2003.

12. Paul A. Volcker Jr. interview, 2003.

13. Ibid.

14. Emmett J. Rice interview, 2003.

15. Paul A. Volcker and Toyoo Gyohten, *Changing Fortunes* (New York: Times Books, 1992), p. 168.

16. Stephen H. Axilrod interview, 2003.

17. John Vinocur, "2 Countries Agree to Bolster Dollar; U.S. and West German Economic Strategists Plan to Intervene in Foreign Money Market," *The New York Times,* September 30, 1979, p. 13.

18. Volcker and Gyohten, *Changing Fortunes,* p. 168.

19. Clyde H. Farnsworth, "A Message from Germany," *The New York Times,* October 7, 1979, p. F17.

20. Volcker and Gyohten, *Changing Fortunes,* p. 168.

21. Robert A. Bennett, "Dollar Plummets in Heavy Trading; Gold at High Again," *The New York Times,* October 2, 1979, p. A1.

22. Paul A. Volcker Jr. interview, 2003.

23. Ibid.

24. Peter D. Sternlight interview, 2003.

25. Paul A. Volcker Jr. interview, 2003.

26. William Greider, *Secrets of the Temple: How the Federal Reserve Runs the Country* (New York, Simon & Schuster, 1989), p. 119–120.

27. Ibid., p. 120.

28. Paul A. Volcker Jr. interview, 2003.

29. Volcker and Gyohten, *Changing Fortunes,* p. 169.

30. Ibid, p. 169.

31. Emmett J. Rice interview, 2003.

32. Greider, *Secrets of the Temple,* p. 122.

33. Volcker and Gyohten, *Changing Fortunes,* p. 169.

34. Greider, *Secrets of the Temple,* p. 123.

35. Joseph R. Coyne interview, 2003.

36. Steven Rattner, "Anti-Inflation Plan by Federal Reserve Increases Key Rate," *The New York Times,* October 7, 1979, p. 1.

37. Bradley Graham, "Gold Soars to $440, then Falls Sharply in Frenzied Trading," *The Washington Post,* October 3, 1979, p. A7.

38. Steven Rattner, "U.S. Money Plan Called Reaction to Speculation," *The New York Times,* October 8, 1979, p. A1.

39. John M. Geddes, "Europeans Mixed over Fed Action," *The New York Times,* October 8, 1979, p. D6.

40. Steven Rattner, "Anti-Inflation Plan by Federal Reserve Increases Key Rate," *The New York Times,* October 7, 1979, p. 1.

41. Hobart Rowen, "Reaction to the Fed; Dollar Rises, Gold Falls $11.50," *The Washington Post,* October 9, 1979, p. F1.

42. James L. Rowe Jr., "Prime Lending Rate Leaps to 14½%; Short-Term Interest up; Prime, Short-Term Rates Skyrocket," *The Washington Post,* October 10, 1979, p. B1.

43. John H. Allan, "Major Banks Raise Loan Rate to 14½%; Stocks off by 26.45," *The New York Times,* October 10, 1979, p. A1.

44. Ibid. See also Rowe, "Prime Lending Rate Leaps to 14½%."

45. Paul A. Volcker Jr. interview, 2003.

46. Peter T. Kilborn, "Volcker Suggests Federal Reserve May Shift Tactics," *The New York Times,* October 10, 1982, p. 1.

47. Ibid.

9. The Fallout

1. Dee Wedemeyer, "Gloomy Gathering of Builders," *The New York Times,* January 25, 1982, p. D1.

2. Allen Sinai interview, 2003.

3. Warren E. Buffett interview, 2003.

4. Joseph E. Stiglitz interview, 2003.

5. Eric Gelman with Rich Thomas and Nikki Finke Greenberg in Washington and Bill Powell in New York, "American's Money Master," *Newsweek*, February 24, 1986, p. 51.

6. Ibid., p. 50.

7. Public Papers of the Presidents of the United States, Jimmy Carter, Remarks and a Question-and-Answer Session with Local Residents in Lansdowne, Pennsylvania, October 2, 1980, p. 2040. See also Clyde H. Farnsworth, "Volcker Criticized by Carter on Rates," *The New York Times*, October 3, 1980, p. A1.

8. Donald H. May, United Press International, Washington, Friday, October 3, 1980, AM cycle.

9. Steven Rattner, "Volcker Critical of Fast Rate Rises; Money Supply, in Reversal, Drops," *The New York Times*, October 4, 1980, p. 1.

10. Ibid.

11. Associated Press, "Ford Raps Carter in Fed Criticism," Saddle Brook, NJ, Friday, October 3, 1980, AM cycle.

12. Donald H. May, United Press International, Washington, October 3, 1980, AM cycle.

13. Dave Goldberg, Associated Press, "Dissatisfaction with Carter Key to Reagan Strength," New York, Tuesday, November 4, 1980, AM cycle.

14. Adam Clymer, "Pool Shows Iran and Economy Hurt Carter among Late-shifting Voters," *The New York Times*, November 16, 1980, p. 1.

15. Stuart E. Eizenstat, *Imperfect Justice: Looted Assets, Slave Labor and the Unfinished Business of World War II* (New York: Public Affairs, Perseus Books Group, 2003), p. 70.

16. Public Papers of the Presidents of the United States, Ronald

Reagan, The President's News Conference, January 19, 1982, p. 36.

17. Public Papers of the Presidents of the United States, Ronald Reagan, The President's News Conference, February 18, 1982, p. 181.

18. George J. Church, reported with David Beckwith and Gisela Bolte in Washington, with other U.S. bureaus, "Paying More for Money; Interest Rates Are Hurting, but Volcker Holds Fast against Inflation," *Time,* March 8, 1982, p. 74.

19. "Regan Doesn't Mind Cigars," Associated Press, Monday, January 25, 1982, AM cycle.

20. Donald T. Regan, *For the Record* (New York, San Diego, London: Harcourt Brace Jovanovich, 1988), p. 172–173.

21. Jonathan Fuerbringer, "Volcker Performance: No Reagan Complaints," *The New York Times,* April 28, 1983, p. D1.

22. Ibid.

23. "A Swelling Chorus of Volcker Boosters," *Business Week,* March 28, 1983, p. 36.

24. Ibid.

25. Public Papers of the Presidents of the United States, Ronald Reagan, Radio Address to the Nation on the Federal Reserve Board Chairman, the Seventh Space Shuttle Flight, and Science Education, June 19, 1983, p. 887. See also Harry Anderson with Thomas M. DeFrank and Rich Thomas in Washington, Kim Foltz and Hope Lampert in New York, and bureau reports, "Volcker: Man for the Moment," *Newsweek,* June 27, 1983, p. 66.

26. David Hoffman and Juan Williams, "President Retains Volcker at Helm of Federal Reserve," *The Washington Post,* June 19, 1983, p. A1.

27. Harry Anderson with Thomas M. DeFrank and Rich Thomas in Washington, Kim Foltz and Hope Lampert in

New York and bureau reports, "Volcker: Man for the Moment," *Newsweek,* June 27, 1983, p. 66.

28. Walter Shapiro with Rich Thomas, Thomas M. DeFrank, and Eleanor Clift in Washington and Hope Lampert in New York, "Will Reagan Reappoint Volcker?" *Newsweek,* May 23, 1983, p. 23.

29. Ibid.

30. Daniel F. Cuff, "Business People: Volcker Is Supported by Executive Poll," *The New York Times,* June 8, 1983, p. D2.

31. David Hoffman and Caroline Atkinson with contribution from Louis Cannon, "Fed Chief Is Gaining Supporters," *The Washington Post,* June 9, 1983, p. A1.

32. "Why the White House Likes Volcker Better Now," *Business Week,* June 27, 1983, p. 24.

33. David Hoffman and Juan Williams, "President Retains Volcker at Helm of Federal Reserve," *The Washington Post,* June 19, 1983, p. A1.

34. Harry Anderson with Rich Thomas in Washington and Erik Ipsen in New York, "Fed Chairman Warns Congress about Budget Deficits and a 'Catch-22,'" *Newsweek,* July 25, 1983, p. 58.

35. John Greenwald, reported by David Beckwith in Washington and Bruce van Voorst in New York, "Paul Volcker Superstar: The Fed Chairman Must Cool off Money Growth without Halting the Recovery," *Time,* July 25, 1983, p. 50.

36. Ibid. See also transcript of testimony before Senate Committee on Banking, House, and Urban Affairs on renomination of Paul A. Volcker, July 14, 1983, 137 pages. See also Peter T. Kilborn, "Volcker Suggests He May Not Serve Full 4-Year Term," *The New York Times,* July 15, 1983, p. A1.

37. Peter T. Kilborn, "White House Asks Federal Reserve to Avoid Rate Rise," *The New York Times,* July 8, 1983, p. A1.

38. Bob Woodward, *Maestro: Greenspan's Fed and the American Boom* (New York: Simon & Schuster, 2000).
39. Paul A. Volcker Jr. interview, 2003.
40. Ibid.

10. Fly-Fishing

1. Reuters, "Small Firm Snares a Big Name; Volcker Joins Boutique Investment Banker," *The Bergen Record,* March 3, 1988, p. D16.
2. Edwin A. Finn Jr., "When Wolfensohn Talks, Big Business Listens—Carefully," *Forbes,* December 26, 1988, p. 87.
3. James D. Wolfensohn interview, 2003.
4. Finn, "When Wolfensohn Talks, Big Business Listens," p. 87.
5. Jeffrey A. Goldstein interview, 2003.
6. James D. Wolfensohn interview, 2003.
7. Jeffrey A. Goldstein interview, 2003.
8. Ibid.
9. Paul A. Volcker Jr. interview, 2003.
10. James Sterngold, "Volcker, the Deal-Making Professor," *The New York Times,* March 3, 1988, p. D1.
11. Ibid.
12. Jim Volcker interview, 2003.
13. Ibid.
14. James D. Wolfensohn interview, 2003.
15. Judith Miller, "Chrysler: The Anatomy of a Loan: Chrysler's Financial Status," *The New York Times,* June 29, 1980, p. 1, Sunday business section.
16. James D. Wolfensohn interview, 2003.
17. Ibid.
18. Alex Brummer, "The People's Plutocrat," *The Guardian,* June 12, 1999, Guardian Art Pages, p. 6. See also Deepak

Gopinath, "Wolfensohn Agonistes," *Institutional Investor International Edition,* September 1, 2000, p. 32.

19. John Berry and Steve Coll, "Volcker Takes Wall Street, Teaching Jobs," *The Washington Post,* March 3, 1988, p. E1.

20. Sterngold, "Volcker, the Deal-Making Professor," p. D1.

21. Volcker and the author had the following exchange about his starting pay at Wolfensohn in his New York office on November 12, 2003:

    Q. There are newspaper stories that say you started for a million dollars a year at Wolfensohn. Others say you got at least $2 million a year.

    A. Well, that depended upon the profitability of the firm.

    Q. Yes, but the impression I have is that there wasn't any time when the profitability fell below a level that would provide you $1 million or $2 million.

    A. Well, it was probably true, but I don't know that it's literally true.

22. Edwin A. Finn Jr., "Down from the Mountain," *Forbes,* December 26, 1988, p. 88.

23. Ibid.

24. Paul A. Volcker Jr. interview, 2003.

25. Finn, "Down from the Mountain," p. 88.

26. Paul A. Volcker and Toyoo Gyohten, *Changing Fortunes* (New York: Times Books, 1992).

27. Ibid.

28. Paul A. Volcker Jr. interview, 2003.

29. Wire report, "Volcker to Take an Active Role in New Venture with Fuji Bank," *The Journal of Commerce,* March 15, 1989, p. 3A.

30. Daniel F. Cuff, "Making a Difference: Volcker's Newest Venture," *The New York Times,* March 15, 1992, p. 10, section 3.

31. James D. Wolfensohn interview, 2003.

32. Jill Dutt, "Banking's Acquiring Mind: At Bankers Trust, Newman Engineers Change He Advocated at Treasury," *The Washington Post,* April 20, 1997, p. H1.
33. Kevin L. McQuaid, "A Titan Grows in Gotham," *The Baltimore Sun,* April 13, 1997, p. 1D. See also Saul Hansell, "Bankers Trust to Acquire Wolfensohn," *The New York Times,* May 23, 1986, p. D1.
34. Hansell, "Bankers Trust to Acquire Wolfensohn."
35. Jeffrey A. Goldstein interview, 2003. See also Paul Volcker, quoted in Stephen Neish, "Boutiques for Sale," *Euromoney,* October, 1996, p. 57–60.
36. Paul A. Volcker Jr. interview, 2003.
37. Saul Hansell, "Market Place: Renaissance Man; Head of Bankers Trust Deftly Guides Turnaround," *The New York Times,* April 18, 1997, p. 1D.
38. Jeffrey A. Goldstein interview, 2003.
39. Bloomberg Business News, "Bankers Trust to Pay $210 Million for Wolfensohn," *The New York Times,* July 23, 1996, p. D4. See also Daniel Kaplan, "Nonbanks Emerge as Acquirer's Most Popular Targets," *The American Banker,* June 11, 1996, p. 25.
40. McQuaid, "A Titan Grows in Gotham."
41. Hansell, "Market Place."
42. Brummer, "The People's Plutocrat," p. 6.
43. Paul A. Volcker Jr. interview, 2003.
44. Paul A. Volcker Jr. interview, 2002.
45. E. Gerald Corrigan interview, 2003.
46. Ibid.
47. Bob Wilson interview, 2003.

Epilogue

1. Anke Dening interview, 2003.
2. Ibid.

3. Paul A. Volcker Jr. interview, 2003.

4. Ibid.

5. "Interview with Paul Volcker," *The Region,* December 1992, posted on the Web at minneapolisfed.org/pubs/region/92-12/int9212.cfm.

Acknowledgments

Many people helped in the creation of this book. Special thanks to Glenn Kramon and William E. Schmidt of *The New York Times*. As a senior editor at John Wiley & Sons, Jeanne Glasser masterfully applied her creativity and skill and turned to Neil Levine for added firepower. My thanks also to Anke Dening, assistant to Paul Volcker, and her colleague, Ann Fivey, Virginia Streitfeld Volcker, Janice Volcker Zima, Jim Volcker, Barbara Dill, Chloe Treaster, Alain Delaqueriere, Stephanie S. Landis, Brent Bowers, Carolyn Wilder, Michelle A. Smith, Andrew Williams, Peter Bakstansky, Robert P. Hartwig, Alison Rea, Rosemary A. Lazenby, Larry J. Robertson, Katherine Malardy, Robert Morrill Jr., Robert D. Hersey Jr., Joyce N. Hershey, Martha L. Connor, Catherine M. Tunis, David W. Skidmore, Peter G. Peterson, Simon Reismann, Werner Schmidt, Sam Cross, Edwin M. Truman, Allen Sinai, Henry Kaufman, Dave Creed, Pedro Rosada, Joan Wulff, Albert Wojnilower, Phyllis Collazo, Marilyn Cervino, Ludmila Kudinova, Jeff Roth, Britt Leckman Peter J. Johnson, Fraser P. Seitel, Suzanne Spellman, Daniel Altman, David Cay Johnston, Saul Hansell, Jonathan D. Glater, Kurt Eichenwald, Peter T. Kilborn, Edmund L. Andrews, Kenneth N. Gilpin, Steven A. Rautenberg, Marvin Wolf, Leslie Sklar, Richard A. Moeller, Donald Stone, Brian DeFiore, Dennis Dalrymple, Melissa Scuereb, Christine Furry, Robyn J. LaMorte, Andrea Gabor, Christine Godek, Marie Jo R. Tirados, Renwick

237

ACKNOWLEDGMENTS

McLean, Nancy M. Shader, Lucille Bertram, Lawrence J. White, Hector R. Perez-Gilbe, Tad Bennifcoff, Judith Higgin, Alan Kardos, Vincent Tortorella, Wei Lee Liu, Cynthia Zimmerly, Chris Campbell, Dan McComas, Sherry Zipp, Amy Rowland, and William P. O'Donnell.

Index